T0128251

THE RIGHT TO NOMINATE

Restoring the Power of the People Over the Power of the Parties

Thomas E. Peterson

authorHOUSE®

AuthorHouse™
1663 Liberty Drive
Bloomington, IN 47403
www.authorhouse.com
Phone: 1 (800) 839-8640

"Eagle and Anchor" cover background illustration copyright (c).
2015 Jake Weidmann, http://www.jakeweidmann.com/

Cover concept, design, and layout by Joshua Farmer, jfjudah@yahoo.com

The Times: A Political Portrait, 1795; "Triumph Government:
perish all its enemies" PR010, #17951;
neg #2737,NewYork Historical Society, (http://www.nyhistory.org)

Published by AuthorHouse: 08/01/2016

ISBN: 978-1-5049-6291-9 (sc)
ISBN: 978-1-5049-6292-6 (hc)
ISBN: 978-1-5049-6171-4 (e)

Library of Congress Control Number: 2015919669

Print information available on the last page.

This book is printed on acid-free paper.

Contents

DILEMMA

We Americans have a magnificent Constitution, truly a landmark in human history.

But under it we have developed a divisive, money-driven, manipulative form of party politics that warps our government, destroys public trust, and miserably squanders the wondrous promise which the birth of America brought into this world.

Why the disparity?

William Gladstone, Prime Minister of Britain, called the American Constitution "the most wonderful work ever struck off at a given time by the brain and purpose of man."[1] He said well.

Given this great foundation, why does every election seem to bring a more intense round of negative ads, hollow speeches, division, manipulation and slander? Why have our elections become a grating process most voters perceive as contemptible, but beyond anyone's ability to change?

And why has our government – intended to be one "of the people, by the people, and for the people", in Lincoln's immortal phrase -- moved beyond the people's ability to correct? What happened to the *sovereignty of the people*, which the Framers based their design on; but which the people now sense is mostly gone?

---

[1] William E. Gladstone, "Kin Beyond Sea," *The North American Review*, September-October 1878, p.185. As quoted in Platt, *Respectfully Quoted*, no. 325, 66.

In this book, we will look carefully at the worldview – the way of thinking -- of the Framers of the Constitution. Our goal will be to re-enter their way of thinking in order to restore and complete their original design.

We will examine lost history: Most Americans today have no idea how intensely the Framers despised political parties (or "factions", as they often called them) when the Constitution was written, nor how often they expressed their loathing for them.

The Framers used words like "**diseases**"[2], "**poison**", "**infection**" and "**taint**" to describe the effects of political parties upon a republic:

"..**diseases**...which have proved fatal to other popular governments, and of which alarming symptoms have been betrayed by our own."
    [*Federalist #14(1)*]

The Framers condemned:
"..that **intolerant spirit** which has **at all times** characterized political parties."
    [*Federalist #1(4)*]

While writing the Constitution, they labored in every part of it to contain and neutralize
"**party divisions**...the **pestilential breath of faction**" which could "**poison** the fountains of justice."
    [*Federalist #81(6)*]

During the great national debate over ratification, the Framers used graphic descriptions of parties to argue for the Constitution to be adopted as a firewall against what they perceived as the gravest internal danger to the new Republic: political parties and factions.

---

[2] NOTE TO THE READER: **Bolding,** *italics,* and **CAPS** have been added to quotations from *The Federalist Papers* for emphasis. The mellifluous writing style of the 18th century makes this remedy needed.

The Worst Enemy

Universally respected first President George Washington warned America against the "spirit of party" in his Farewell Address. In popular forms of government, Washington said, this spirit "is seen in its greatest rankness and is truly their worst enemy."

Thomas Jefferson, who was not present at the Constitutional Convention, nonetheless captured the attitude of the Framers perfectly, saying, "If I could not go to heaven except with a party, I would not go there at all."[3]

This was the worldview which gave birth to the American Constitution.

This worldview not only *produced* the Constitution, but the great national debate over ratification was engaged and won in terms of it. So when Americans chose to make the Constitution the "supreme law of the land", they made that choice in the context of a forcefully argued dire warning from the Framers *against* political parties.

Questions

As we examine this reality of the Framers' worldview, which has not been accurately transmitted by most modern historians – which, in fact, has been glossed over and lost to the majority of Americans-- we will confront unresolved questions:

> When the Framers expressed loathing and distrust for political parties, did that include *our* parties, the ones existing today? Or did they have in mind some trouble-making groups unique to the 1700's?

---

[3] Letter to Francis Hopkinson, March 1789

When we find that they were deliberate and forceful in their censure of parties *whenever and wherever* they make their appearance in a republic (yes, that includes our modern ones); then we will face

More Questions

If the Framers genuinely loathed political parties, considering them inevitable but a source of danger and blight to any free government; if they reluctantly concluded that parties could not be banished without banishing liberty itself; and then devoted enormous effort into designing the Constitution to contain and check such parties (and the ambitious people who lead them); then after two hundred years of party ascendance *contrary to their original design,* isn't it time to look again at what the Framers of the Constitution thought and wrote on the subject? And to squarely face this question: Were they right?

Or more accurately, "Were they right the first time?" – the time during which the Constitution was written and adopted. Because after that, contrary to their own stated principles, a few of the Founders themselves fell into fierce partisanship. In the course of fighting one another, these few Founders ended up generating the very party system they vehemently claimed to loath.

That party system would in turn trash and discard crucial elements of the original Constitutional design.

Naïve?

Were the Framers just naïve at the time of the Constitutional Convention, lacking the experience necessary to understand the role political parties might play in a republic?

OR WERE THEY RIGHT? And are we today eating the same poisoned fruit of partisanship that sent republics of the past into writhing death agonies, one after another? Something the Framers warned might happen to us?

Our examination of their original design -- how they crafted the Constitution to *check* parties, to stop them from taking over our government, along with the reasons they gave for doing so -- will bring up

Greater Questions

If the Framers' aim was to design a freely elected, representative government not dominated by political parties, then what went wrong? What did they think was going to happen? Why would they think elections might be carried out *apart from* party domination?

And if their aim was a representative government that could safely *include* but *not be dominated* by parties, then what happened? To them, and to us? Why didn't this part of their plan work?

But above all: Could their original plan have worked?

COULD IT WORK TODAY?

Could the Framers' original design of a freely elected, representative government that could include but not be controlled by political parties be restored? And begin to function in our time?

What would such a Republic look like? – The one the Framers designed?

Can American state and federal governments be freed from the unchecked control of political parties without destroying – or even infringing – the rights and liberties of party members? How?

On what principles of free, republican government can we restore the Framers' original design?

DEDICATION
This book is dedicated to restoring
the original design
of the American Constitution.

Not for the sake of idealism or sentiment; but because that original design is simply the most brilliant plan of government ever conceived by the human race.

The original design of the Constitution not only captured a great vision of liberty and essential rights, but it also *applied* that vision, creating the practical framework needed to channel and contain the ways men have conducted politics in government for most of recorded history.

It is in this meeting of visionary principles with political reality that the greatness of the Constitution lays. Restoring the Constitution's original design will restore the unlimited potential of the great Republic it was created to protect and promote.

Since the essential elements of the original design are timeless, restoring it will not only give us back our original form of government but will also provide the best and brightest path into our future.

America's marvelous Constitutional design has been tarnished and disgraced by the party system, which originally had *no* place in it. But, as is the case when unchecked growth by a physical tumor displaces healthy tissue, the party system has displaced the Framers' original design.

PART I

CHAPTER ONE

The "Parties-Only" System

Every American living today has grown up under a party system of government. Congress and all our state legislatures have long been controlled by political parties, and by party leaders. As things stand now, no legislation can pass any of our legislatures, state or federal, unless approved by party leaderships. All state and federal expenditures are controlled by these parties and their leaders.

This dominance, this control, handed back and forth between parties, is not the government the Framers designed; it is not what they intended. But contrary to their original design, party control of our governments now stands at close to 100%; and has for as long as anyone alive can remember.

The mental conditioning created by someone's entire lifetime being spent under one political system can form an inner bondage, even if that system is aberrant or dysfunctional; mentally and emotionally fixating that person into the only context they've ever known.

In our case, a lifelong experience of the party, or "parties-**only**", system (i.e., parties only, in control of government) makes it difficult for many of us to even imagine what a true republic might be like apart from party domination.

This same lifelong conditioning, reinforced by weariness and cynicism, makes it difficult for many people to even begin to grasp the thinking that shaped our Constitution: the thinking of the Framers, who gave their utmost to design and bring to birth exactly such a republic: one *not dominated*, not controlled, by political parties. A majority of Americans today react with complete surprise – and sometimes disbelief – when told that this was the conscious goal of the Framers' design.

The first premise of this book is that the Framers were right about the downside of political parties when they wrote the Constitution. They were not naïve. Their reading of history – that virtually all past republics have been pulled apart and *destroyed* by factions; *ruined* by (party-driven) abuse of their treasuries; or *degraded into futility* by bitter partisanship – was correct.

In The Framer's Words:

A survey of the *Federalist Papers,* which James Madison said reflected accurately the thinking of the delegates at the Constitutional Convention of 1787, yields an astonishing list of words and phrases which express the Framers' enmity toward political parties and factions. For example:

> *"tainted"* – "…the unsteadiness and injustice with which a factious spirit has tainted our public administration."
> [*Federalist #10:1*]

> *"prostitutes"* – ".. or whether he prostitutes that advantage [the power of appointment] to the advancement of persons whose chief merit is their implicit devotion to his will and to the support of a despicable and dangerous system of personal influence…"
> [Federalist #77(6)]

> *"poison"* – "A spirit of faction, which is apt to mingle its poison in the deliberations of all bodies of men,…
> [*Federalist #15 (12)*]

"malignity" – "…artificial treasons have been the great engines by which violent factions, the natural offspring of free government, have usually wreaked their alternate malignity on each other…"
[*Federalist #43 (6)*]

"demon" – "it ought not to be forgotten that the demon of faction will, at certain seasons, extend his scepter over all numerous bodies of men."
[*Federalist #65 (10)*]

"pervert" – "…that a spirit of faction may sometimes pervert its deliberations;"
[i.e., the legislature]
[*Federalist #73 (8)*]

Parallels & Comparisons

As eye-opening as these single-word descriptions are, even more is revealed by the parallels and comparisons used by the *Federalist* authors, because they assumed (correctly) that most of their readers would agree with these comparisons, with no explanation required:

"…ambition, avarice, personal animosity, **party** opposition…"
[i.e. negative things which may appear on either side of a debate]
[*Federalist #1 (4)*]

"…a principle of this kind gives greater scope to foreign corruption, as well as to domestic **faction**, than that which permits the sense of the majority to decide…" [*Federalist #22 (10)*]

"..to the security of liberty against the enterprises and assaults of ambition, of **faction**, and of anarchy."
[*Federalist #70 (1)*]

"…republics of Greece and Italy…soon to be overwhelmed
by the tempestuous waves of sedition and **party** rage."
[*Federalist #9 (1)*]

In The Framers' Worldview:

The "spirit" and effects of a **party** mentality are lumped together
over and over in the Framers' writings, and in their public
comments, with the most debased and dehumanizing of traits:
avarice, personal animosity, corruption, raw ambition, anarchy,
sedition and other extremely negative motivations.

The Framers carefully analyzed the historical record of failure –
dismal, often cataclysmic failure -- on the part of past republics,
with the goal of understanding and correcting the root causes.

They concluded that the bitter antagonisms of faction and party
were *the* repeated source of failure in the agonized history of
destroyed republics.

The correction they applied to that record of repeated tragedy
was nothing short of brilliant: the Constitutional design. They
relied upon liberty as the prime solution in a system of checks and
balances, with marvelous results.

The Problem

The Framers of the Constitution were not in any basic error in their
attempt to check and contain the effects of faction, of party, which
brought down so many past republics: *but their design simply did
not extend quite far enough.*

By stopping just short of what was necessary, their marvelous
design left America vulnerable to the corruption and divisiveness
that subsequent generations experienced after un-checked political

parties established a suffocating predominance over American elections.

After the founding of America, the same pattern of unchecked dominance of the electoral process by organized political parties has played out in every free republic established since ours.

This outcome (parties in control of government) is directly opposed to what the Framers aimed for and labored to write into the Constitution.

Historically and functionally, the party system pushed aside and replaced the Framers' original design.

This historic pattern, repeated in many republics, reveals an underlying human reality which the Framers' design, as brilliant as it was, was not quite able to contain. Not because they were in error – they were not. But because there was an element missing from their design; one thing left out.

This crucial element was omitted simply because neither the Framers nor anyone else on earth at that time had had experience with repeated elections in a large free republic.

Two centuries of experience have gradually revealed the nature of the missing element. This element is astonishingly simple, like oxygen in the air we breathe: invisible to the eye but necessary for life.

It is the right to nominate, which has been an unprotected, abused, or missing element in our representative government. Without this right being protected and its use provided for, the people of our republic became like travelers on a winter night allowed to park their car in a garage and sleep in it. They must leave the engine running to stay warm; but the garage doors are closed.

As oxygen is depleted and pollutants build, death creeps close. The survival of these travelers will not depend on their eyesight or their hearing; but on knowledge and understanding. As tired and unfocused as they may feel, they must get out of that garage to live.

And if just enough fresh air to keep them alive is leaking in, but their minds are unclear and their actions impaired, they still must decide to get out of that garage.

The freedom and right to nominate is like oxygen to our republic. When it is limited; or allowed only in a selective manner, we are being stifled politically. Artificial limits and selective applications imposed against our Right to nominate, for the benefit of a tiny minority, are today the greatest internal threat to American liberty that exists.

Many people sense today that our Republic is somehow at stake, without knowing exactly why. But the 'feeling' is accurate. Something is going on that is taking our Republic to the brink of failure; but we have not had the vocabulary to even describe what is happening to us, let alone correct it.

The reason is that there has been a missing Right of the people, unredeemed and unprotected, which has been exploited by a few at the great expense of the many. This undefended human right is as simple as oxygen, but like other basic human rights, is difficult to see: it is the right to nominate.
Not only is it the *right* of the people to nominate candidates for public office; but civic health in any true republic eventually depends on the people *exercising* this right independent of the government and independent of all political parties or interest groups.

Unless the people hold and **independently** exercise their right to nominate, then republican governments must fail, sooner or later. Their failure comes through a process of debasement: being gradually changed until government is no longer controlled by the people, but by powerful individuals and by organized groups which can manipulate the people through *their* control of nominations for public office.

By being overlooked, the Right to Nominate has been unredeemed; neglected and not provided for. Being unredeemed, this right has been usurped by a variety of organized groups in different societies, including religious mullahs, military juntas, and tyrannical single-Party systems.

Axiom

It is an axiom that in a republic (an elective system),

> *"Whoever controls nominations for elective offices controls the resulting government."*

This hidden lever of control rightfully belongs to the people.

Without this Right being *held* [through Constitutional guarantee] and *exercised* by the people, then it is inevitable that some individual or organized group will step in to do the nominating of candidates for office.

Control of government then will *transfer* (suddenly, as it did in Iran; or gradually, as happened in most modern republics) from the people to the group or groups controlling nominations. With this transfer of control comes a diminishment or total loss of the rightful sovereignty of the people.

In obvious cases, such as ruling mullahs, military juntas or single-party tyrannies, taking control from the people is a planned, deliberate act; the result of conspiracy. Such a government is illegitimate; it is not drawn from the will of the people and can only be maintained by force.

But in America, this transfer of control over government from the people to organized parties did not happen directly as a result of conspiracy, or through evil intent; but rather through evolving electoral customs that appeared to be voluntary.

The Right to Nominate was latent in the early days of our republic, unrecognized and unredeemed. Because it was unprotected and seemed available, no one stopped to question, "Might this belong to the people?" or, "Should we just be *taking* this?"

Instead, like opportunists exploiting a natural resource, party enthusiasts simply laid hold of the unprotected Right and used it for themselves and their allies. They were not purposely doing wrong; the Framers had inadvertently left this door open.

If the Framers had recognized this right, they would never have considered denying it to any American, party member or not.

Amendment IX in the Bill of Rights makes it powerfully clear that the Founders were a.) aware that they may not have covered every Right that belonged to the people; and were b.) adamant in a way that only those victorious in war can be, that any such un-described Right was "off limits"—retained by the people.[4]

What they would have done (had they been aware of this right) would be to ensure that all Americans could exercise it, not just a few in elite positions; because they would have foreseen the result: that control of the government would devolve upon those few who controlled nominations.

That is exactly what happened during the early days of our Republic.

---

[4] **AMENDMENT IX—"THE ENUMERATION IN THE CONSTITUTION OF CERTAIN RIGHTS SHALL NOT BE CONSTRUED TO DENY OR DISPARAGE OTHERS RETAINED BY THE PEOPLE."**

Later we will examine how the hard-fought reforms leading to the establishment of primary elections, in spite of high hopes, failed to return control of government to the people. (Why? Because virtually all persons running in primaries are party members; so virtually all nominees emerging from those primaries will be what? Party candidates. So control of government stays in the hands of parties and party leaders.)

The historical fact that American political parties, with their ferocious energy, were able to trample over and defeat most of the Framers' Constitutional restraints on them does not prove the Framers wrong.

It only shows that something was missing from their design, a factor unknown to them which would give what they held in contempt -- *"party spirit"*-- first a foothold; then a dominant role; and finally, complete control of American government.

CHAPTER TWO

Lost History

Before we can discover exactly what was missing from the Framers' design, we must first recover the history of the design itself, a history lost to most Americans.

The great pitfall, the sin, of historians is to project modern ways of thinking, or intervening developments, backwards onto an earlier time.

In the case of early America, there is the complicating reality that several of the Founders themselves (including three of the intellectual powerhouses: Hamilton, Jefferson, and Madison) fell into conflict and then into heated partisanship in the 1790's, after the Constitution was adopted. Contrary to their own stated principles, they ended up founding the first American political parties, though they were long reluctant to admit that fact. ("Party" continued for many years to be a dirty word, an insult used to smear opponents.)

This historic fall of several of the Founders into partisanship has produced a stumbling block for historians, leading many of them to gloss over or explain away the strong anti-party convictions which animated virtually all the Framers at the time of writing the Constitution.

After all, these historians have reasoned, if some of the Founders appeared to think differently in the decades after Ratification; or acted in ways contrary to their previous convictions, shouldn't we assume that those earlier convictions didn't ultimately mean much? And were simply doomed to be discarded?

One such historian dismisses the worldview of the Framers while they crafted the Constitution in a single casual phrase, saying that after Ratification, they "…came down off their pedestals…" [i.e., down into the nasty realities of partisan politics]. He thus supplies in one stroke his grand historical judgment that a.) the triumph of partisanship must have been inevitable (since it happened); and b.) the Framers of the Constitution prior to that occurrence must have dwelt in some "pedestal" state, and therefore held unrealistic views of representative government which he, and we, are wiser to ignore.

Exactly how the Framers could produce the American Constitution from such a naïve, unrealistic viewpoint, this historian does not bother to explain.

In this approach to history, the worldview of the Framers – the worldview which gave us the Constitution – is dismissed as a set of "earlier ideas" not worth real study because those ideas were about to be trampled into oblivion anyway by the "brutal realities" of the "developing modern political system".

So even if those "earlier ideas" were what produced the American Constitution, shouldn't they now be re-interpreted or 'understood' in terms of what we ended up with: the party system? (i.e., parties-*only*, controlling government)?

Or perhaps the **parties-only** system itself, in this revised view of history, should be looked upon as an "unintended achievement" of the Founders, in spite of their deep convictions and vehement statements to the contrary.

The Fall

The party system, seen from the Framers' worldview, was not an "achievement": it was a terrible failure, a Fall of epic proportions.

A few key Founders slipped and fell from the height of political vision and clarity that prevailed in Philadelphia at the Constitutional Convention of 1787. By their fall, they brought ruin to crucial parts of the Constitution's original design.

From the height reached in Philadelphia at the Convention, a height rarely seen in human history, these men fell into the same yawning chasms of rivalry, enmity and bitter conflict that throughout history has brought ruin to the human race.

As they fell, wrestling and thrashing each other, they also slammed shut the window of civility that had enabled the Constitution to be written.

How did this happen? What process or series of events led *a few* of the Founders – namely Thomas Jefferson, Alexander Hamilton, and James Madison -- to go from detesting the very concept of "party" to actually founding the first organized *major* parties in America, however reluctant they were to admit it?

Before the Fall

The parties which stirred the loathing of nearly all the leaders of the American Revolution were basic in nature: **1.**) local or state-based pockets of influence formed around strong personalities; **2.**) what today we would call "special-interests" – groups coalesced around local and regional economic interests such as: farmers in western Pennsylvania, New England shippers, or Virginia planters; and **3.**) the factions of history, rooted in human nature and manifested by fastening political identity onto ethnicity, family alliances, a shared ideology or a common cause.

These were the "factions" that had torn apart republic after republic in centuries past; and in the Framers' sober estimate, could easily do so again.

Such repeated historic disasters, by the mid-1700's, had left republican government itself in disrepute among educated persons, despite its appeal as a political theory. The image of a "republic", by that time, was permeated by the historical stink of agony and failure. Past republics had shown a consistent pattern of ending up in a ditch, often violently; and this terrible pattern was primarily due to the deadly operations of faction and party.

The Segmented Rattlesnake

What drew the enmity of the Framers toward factions and parties in their own time was the conduct shown by various groups during the War of Independence; and then again during the years following that war, under the Articles of Confederation. During the war, the Continental Army suffered horrendous shortages of men, supplies, and equipment; not because there was a shortage of those things in the country – America was already one of the most prosperous places on earth[5] – but mostly because of Congress' inability to overcome resistance and quarreling from different parties in the states.

Worse, there were individuals and groups who sympathized with, and sometimes supplied the British. One of George Washington's challenges while the Continental Army encamped in New Jersey was the constant need to patrol the roads to interdict food wagons on their way from local farmers to the British army.

In the safety and comfort we enjoy today, we may forget that the men we call "Founders" were leaders of a rebellion against a worldwide empire, the greatest military Power of their time. Their cause looked to be in more or less desperate straits for over six years. During most of that time, these leaders faced death by hanging as the most likely reward for their efforts.

---

[5] Collier and Collier, *Decision in Philadelphia,* 29.

Petty quarrels and jealousies within the States, along with disunity and selfish demands from local parties -- all of which seriously hampered the war effort and endangered their Cause -- earned the profound loathing of the Founding leadership.

A Simmering Chaos

After overcoming the effects of disunity and lack of supply during the War, the Founding leaders again encountered parties and factions playing an abusive role under the Articles of Confederation.

A sort of low-level chaos prevailed during this post-war time, with no effective means to resolve trade or border disputes between states. These disputes often boiled down to clashes between interest groups (read "parties"). Parties in one state would regularly clash with the parties and/or government of another state, especially when taxes or tariffs were involved.

This intense clash of interests did not occur in a friendly atmosphere; nor in the context of national unity. Instead, the lack of effective government tended to increasingly dissolve whatever sense of being one country still remained after the Revolution; to the extent that clear-eyed men saw the probability of a breakup of the states into regional groupings which at some point could end up in armed confrontations with each other.[6]

In short, state and local interest groups (**parties)** were producing nasty conflicts that threatened to undo what the War of Independence had gained. They were bringing the new American republic, under its Articles of Confederation, to the brink of falling apart. As a result, they were also presenting the spectacle

---

[6]   *The Federalist Papers, #7*; Alexander Hamilton

of America to the rest of the world as simply another "basket-case republic" lurching toward failure.

These war and postwar experiences were powerful fuel for the Framers' profoundly negative attitude toward factions and parties, heading into the Philadelphia Convention of 1787.

The Reason the Constitution Was Written

These experiences under the Articles of Confederation have led to nearly unanimous agreement that intense discord and conflict *between parties and interests* in the several states were what provoked the Federal Convention to be called and the Constitution to be written. It was written to keep these intense clashes of interest from breaking the young country apart.

More of the Framers' Worldview

An added factor in the Framers' approach toward parties was that many of them shared the experience of a classical education[7], which included familiarity with the great thinkers of Western civilization. It also included knowledge of ancient and Renaissance republics, a knowledge base they referred to many times with one another. They were well acquainted with the fact that a majority of those historic republics experienced agonizing deaths after being torn apart by factions.

At the Height: The Summer of '87

The net result was that the Framers entered the Convention with an intelligent and principled ***anti***-party mentality. It was from this mentality that they designed and wrote the Constitution. Their

---

[7] Collier and Collier, *Decision in Philadelphia,* 54.

motivation was not to destroy parties (because, as they clearly saw, that would be to destroy liberty itself). Their motivation was to *constrain*; to channel and contain the *effects*[8] of party, to keep parties from dominating or destroying the new Republic.

One of the most remarkable features of the Constitutional Convention of 1787 was a phenomenon impressed on the minds of those present; to which they made reference in later years. They spoke of an atmosphere present at the Convention, occasioned by deep concern over the crisis engulfing the infant republic (and threatening to end it), which helped to produce an unusual depth of collaboration among the delegates.

That atmosphere was encouraged and sustained – some thought even produced -- by the presence of George Washington. So great was the gratitude and respect felt toward Washington in the country, that John Adams once fumed that it bordered on adoration, on worship. But Adams, like every other national leader of the time, also held Washington in his highest esteem; based, in Jefferson's phrase, "on merit".

Washington's agreement to chair the Convention (and his behind-the-scenes encouragement for calling it) was widely seen as its seal of approval; as almost a guarantee of some level of success.

While Washington purposely took little part in discussions, his presence and the enormous respect in which he was held had a profound impact on the conduct of the Convention. One effect of Washington's presence was to make personal pettiness between delegates virtually unthinkable. The same went for partisan barbs; not because Washington had to actively repress them, but because the men present knew that such things would simply bring embarrassment to all.

---

[8]   *Federalist #10, (3-5)*

With Washington presiding, the experienced leaders who came to Philadelphia found freedom to function at their highest level; and the Convention settled in for its great work.

The Federal Convention of 1787 became a shining exception to the history of failure connected to such gatherings; a rare moment remarkably "exempt" (in James Madison's words) from the pettiness and entrenched ill will of "**parties**".

CHAPTER THREE

The Great Design

What were the realities fashioned in Philadelphia in the summer of '87? How were parties viewed and treated in the Constitution's original design? Let's put aside the tainted views of revisionist historians, and rediscover the words of the Framers themselves.

The Federalist Papers were written by Alexander Hamilton and James Madison, with a few additions from John Jay, to explain and promote the proposed new Constitution during the great debate over its ratification.

In *Federalist #37,* James Madison wrote (in third person, under the pseudonym "Publius") about the history of "deliberative bodies", and then presented what was actually an insider's view of the Federal Convention:[9]

> "The history of almost all the great councils and consultations held among mankind for reconciling their discordant opinions, assuaging their mutual jealousies and adjusting their respective interests, is a history of **factions,** contentions, and disappointments, and may be classed among the most dark and degrading pictures which display the infirmities and depravities of the human character."
> [*Federalist #37(15)*]

But in contrast, "Publius"/Madison went on to say,

> "...we are necessarily led to two important conclusions. The first is that the convention must have enjoyed, in a

---

[9]   In all citations, **bolding** is added.

very singular degree, an exemption from **the pestilential influence of party animosities – the disease most incident to deliberative bodies and most apt to contaminate their proceedings."**

[*ibid*]

Madison was not suggesting that there weren't enormous issues in play at the Federal Convention; issues which could have resulted in a permanent rupture and would have condemned the Convention to the ash heap of history. Nor was he suggesting that there were not enormous differences in viewpoint among the delegates. James Madison, perhaps better than anyone, knew the opposite to be true.

What Madison described as being largely absent from the Convention were not great issues nor serious differences of opinion, but "animosities"; specifically, the entrenched ill will he called "party animosities".

A Glorious Exchange

The result was (to use an appropriate 18th century phrase), a *glorious exchange*. Glorious because of the freedom present for delegates to speak their minds with candor, without fear of merely provoking enmity from other delegates; and to speak with passion about what each one thought might be vital to the final design, without provoking party rancor.

It was a glorious exchange, indeed; conducted under a pledge of confidentiality from all the delegates, with a remarkable degree of freedom and honesty. There were enormous strains, due to the greatness of the issues and to vastly differing views. But the strains were honest ones, and were able to be overcome *because of* the Convention's remarkable freedom from the pettiness and ill-will of party spirit.

So the Constitutional Convention fervently debated the greatest issues of its time; indeed, some of the greatest issues of all time; but with a candor and honesty that was due to a "singular degree of exemption" (in Madison's words) from that **rankest** of spirits (Washington's description), "**party animosity**".

The Foulest Element

It is this "**rank spirit**", this foulest element of the human psyche, which twists civil debate and honest differences of opinion into contempt, slander, bitter anger and malice among men.

This same foul trait, in intensified form, captures the psyche of murderers; and turns objective differences among men into the maelstrom of war. It is this awful human trait that occasionally erupts into ethnic violence wherein men hack and club their own neighbors to death.

Closer to home it is this same rank trait, this terrible failure in human nature, which ruins so many marriages, turning what once were havens of affection into barred prisons fouled by open running sewers of anger, bitterness, misery and pain.

The Framers of the Constitution were anything but naïve.

When they described this "dark and degrading" tendency in human nature, this "disease"; this "poison" which can so easily creep into civic affairs through factions, through party spirit, they knew whereof they spoke.

Realism

Under no illusion that human nature might be changed by a mere piece of paper, or by floods of rhetoric, the delegates who came to the convention in Philadelphia listened to a piece of timeless and realistic advice for doing their work. It was a saying often attributed to James Madison, but which actually cropped up frequently in articles and sermons of the time and almost surely predated Madison. But it was an accurate, powerful summary of the Framers' working mentality:

"We must take men as we find them."

Thankfully, the Framers were practical, experienced leaders[10]; not hand wringers who would go about pleading for everyone to "be nice". They set out to construct a government that might *contain* (and so partially neutralize) some of the most dangerous forces in human nature – forces manifested within nations through factions and parties -- by balancing one competing interest against another, thus checking them both.

Dividing the government into three branches; and the Legislature into two houses were, of course, the most enduring parts of their design, intended to insure that no single individual or faction could gain control of the whole government.

But that was just the beginning.

To understand and *restore* their design, we must dig into the details, the specifics of it; and examine the reasoning they used to create it.

Those who at first may be offended by the phrase "anti-party" in the following examination, thinking it too strong, need only reflect on the list of descriptive words used by the Framers themselves about parties ("poison", "disease", "pestilence", "taint", "infect", etc.) and ask themselves, "How much more 'anti' could anyone possibly have been?"

---

[10] All 55 delegates had held office or worked in government positions. Collier and Collier, *Decision in Philadelphia,*103.

CHAPTER FOUR

The Original Design

Anti-Party Clause #1

THE HOUSE OF REPRESENTATIVES:
NO CONTINUITY

As most of us learned, the Framers at the Federal Convention designed the House of Representatives to be elected every two years to insure that the Representatives "stayed close to the people".

What most of us didn't learn was why they decided to have the *whole* House up for election in each cycle, instead of staggering terms to provide legislative continuity, as they did with the Senate.

In fact, a *lack* of continuity in the House was what the Framers were after.

They wanted the whole House elected again every 2 years:

> "..both as a security against the perpetuation of the same spirit in the body, and AS A CURE FOR THE DISEASES OF FACTION."
> *[Federalist #61(4)]*

As experienced leaders, they well understood that:

> "..the spirit of **PARTY** in different degrees must be expected to **INFECT** all political bodies," *[Federalist #26(10)]* and,

> "..it ought not to be forgotten that the **DEMON OF FACTION** will, at certain seasons, extend his scepter over all numerous bodies of men."
> *[Federalist #65(10)]*

This plan for electing the whole House anew each cycle was their attempt to prevent the "**infection**", the "**disease**" of party spirit from being passed on from one Congress to the next; and thus exorcise the "**demon of faction**".

They hoped that a fresh infusion of newly elected citizen candidates would break up party cabals. And they anticipated that there would be enough persons of integrity in each new class of Representatives to be able to derail – or at least pass a fresh judgment upon -- any ongoing party plans.

Two things are worthy of note:

First, the advent of organized *major* political parties (as opposed to the interest groups and personality-based parties most familiar to the Framers) made mincemeat out of this provision.

The *organized* parties were fully intent on passing their "spirit" from one Congress to the next, with the goal of controlling Congress, period.

This part of the original design, so well conceived for maintaining a government *"of the people and by the people"*, was quickly trampled into uselessness by the ferocious energy of the emerging, *organized* major parties.

The Guideline

Second (*and of utmost importance*) was that, in their attempt to prevent the House from falling under the ongoing domination of parties, the Framers *turned to the people* as the natural counterbalance, the "group" with rightful sovereignty; and therefore with sufficient vested interest in checking or controlling such a development as to bring about a decisive, enduring balance of power.

This feature of their original design, i.e., their reliance *on the people* to act on their own behalf as the overruling, natural counterbalance to party influences in government must be our guideline as well, as we seek to restore the original design of the American Constitution.

"But hasn't that proven inadequate?" someone might ask.

No! When the people redeem what rightfully belongs to them, the Right to Nominate their own candidates for public office -- apart from and independent of all parties -- along with the means to do so; it will bring an end to the ***exclusivity*** of that hidden lever of power (to nominate) which the parties have surreptitiously used for so long to take the reins of government away from the people.

When the Right to Nominate is fully redeemed by the people: enshrined in every constitution, state and federal; then the Framers' wonderfully balanced Constitutional design will be restored. And finally be able to function.

The sovereignty of the people, which they are *so* unhappy about losing (though the fact that this is the cause of their unhappiness is not yet a public understanding); the rightful sovereignty which they are *so uneasy* about missing under the rule of parties, will be restored.

The Framers' marvelous design, which counted on the people to play a policy-governing, decisive supervisory role to counterbalance the selfish, client-based effects of parties, will be vindicated.

Of..., By..., and For...WHOM?

The Framers assumed that parties will exist whenever and wherever there is free elective government.

One great task of Constitutional design therefore, as they saw it, was to ensure that the interests of the people, and of the country as a whole, are able to prevail over the competing, narrower claims of political parties[11] (and their clients); and to prevail over claims through parties from interest groups or ideological camps.

A good constitutional Design, in the Framers' view, must ensure that the people are able to exercise sovereignty, to compel the adjustment or denial of these various claims, through their elected representatives.

This is what the Framers aimed for; this was their conscious goal.

In short, (using their language) their design attempted to insure that the people, through their elected representatives, should ***rule over all parties,*** making sovereign decisions among their competing claims.

Never did they intend or think that parties should take control of the government and ***rule over the people.***

But by usurping the power to nominate [not in itself wrong – parties have the same right to nominate candidates as do other private clubs, groups, or individuals – no more, and no less], in such a way that it became customary to limit available candidates to their own members—a trend institutionalized by primaries--and thus leave the people out of the initial selection process, the parties transformed the *peoples' representatives* into *party representatives*. They quietly gained a perpetual lock on elective offices and, as a result, perpetual control of government.

This principle: that the people, through *their* elected representatives should rule over all parties, underlies the Framers' entire design. Based on the people's sovereignty, this principle is foundational to

---

[11] *The Federalist #10,* James Madison

all the specific provisions which they wrote into the Constitution designed to *check* and *contain* party influences.

The Framers were not simplistically or "mindlessly" anti-party. They knew what they were about. They were designing the government for a great and lasting Republic, a government which could *include* parties, but would **be** a government *"..of the people, by the people, and for the people"*, in Lincoln's later immortal phrase.

They emphatically did NOT intend to design a government...*of the parties, by the parties, and for the parties' clients and special interests."*

Anti-Party Clause #2

THE PRESIDENTIAL VETO:
AGAINST THE EFFECTS OF FACTION

It is sadly ironic that we think of the President's veto largely in terms of party agendas, i.e., as enabling a minority party in the presidency to check the power of a majority party in Congress. This is history revised (and thus falsified) by the writers of civics textbooks.

The irony of this false understanding lies in fact that the Framers' intention for the veto power was, First, that the executive branch should be able to "defend itself", under the Separation of Powers in the three branch system; but Second, that the veto should be in place to stop any mere party agenda (or other "wrong impulse") from affecting legislation at all. The laws, they reasoned, were to be for the good of the whole community:

> "...upon the supposition that the legislature will not be infallible; that the love of power may sometimes betray it into a disposition to encroach upon the rights of other members of the government; that a **SPIRIT OF FACTION** may sometimes **PERVERT** its

deliberations; that impressions of the moment may sometimes hurry it into measures which itself, on maturer reflection, would condemn."

[Federalist #73(8)]

"It [the veto] establishes a salutary check upon the legislative body, calculated to guard the community **AGAINST** the **EFFECTS OF FACTION,** precipitancy, or of any impulse unfriendly to the common good, which may happen to influence a majority of that body."

[Federalist #73(6)]

With the triumph of the party system, this magisterial power of veto, meant for protecting the community *against* the effects of faction or party, was captured *by* the parties and pressed into service as a political weapon, a bludgeon to use in party battles.

Above Party

The Framers, while laboring at the Convention, had George Washington in clear prospect as the probable first President who might wield this veto power. So they had good reason to hope, as they wrote the Constitution, that the presidency would normally be occupied by leaders who were "above party", not creatures of it; and who should be able to veto any future legislation enacted through party influences for the benefit of party clients or party interests.

We can be thankful that we have the words of the Framers themselves to cut through "spin", through the arguments of party apologists and failed historians, so that we may understand the Framers' intentions for virtually every paragraph and phrase they wrote into the Constitution.

The veto was intended to protect America *against* parties, and against their effects. It was intended to guard against all parties, all the time.

Anti-Party Clause #3

THE JUDICIAL BRANCH:
SO PARTIES DON'T "POISON THE FOUNTAINS OF JUSTICE"

We celebrate the wisdom of the Framers in dividing government into three independent branches. But we seldom hear the details of their reasoning.

The British constitution places their highest judicial authority squarely in the House of Lords, the upper house of Parliament. After describing several drawbacks to this arrangement (the same men both passing laws, then deciding their application; the lack of judicial temperament and/or training in some legislators, etc.), the most devastating of the Framers' reasons for a separate judicial branch is rendered in *Federalist #81*:

> "...on account of the natural propensity of such bodies [i.e., legislatures] to **PARTY DIVISIONS,** there will be no less reason to fear that the **PESTILENTIAL BREATH OF FACTION MAY POISON THE FOUNTAINS OF JUSTICE."**
> *[Federalist #81(6)]*

In the Framers' original design, part of the reason for having a third Branch of government was to keep party politics, and party spirit, out of the Judiciary and out of the decisions of the courts. They understood that the spirit of partisanship would inevitably pervert, or destroy altogether, the impartiality required of a court.

This memorable phrase, **"THE PESTILENTIAL BREATH OF FACTION"**, captures the attitude of the Framers toward parties. The "breath of faction" didn't simply smell a bit bad; its smell was foul because its source was a disease; and that disease could be passed on, could "poison" the recipient. This phrase is one of many used in the *Federalist Papers* to describe something the Framers knew well, and detested: "party spirit".

"The Pestilential Breath of Party"
vs.
The Three-Branch Design

So what can we say about our parties today, which periodically "fight like hell" trying to gain control of all three Branches of the government at once? How is it that a U.S. Senator might lecture at a university in the morning about the "great safety and wisdom of the Separation of Powers" in our Constitution; and then go fight in the afternoon, with all his energy, to breach that design, and overcome it, so that his party might control all three Branches?

Suppose some party leader had announced, soon after the Constitution was ratified,

"Now that we have this great protection of the Separation of Powers in our Constitution, our party wishes to announce that we will dedicate ourselves to overcoming and *defeating* this design, in order to gain control over the whole government, so that our great and wonderful agenda for this country may finally be <u>irrevocably</u> established!! And so that the despicable forces behind the deluded people who oppose us don't get hold of it first, and *ruin* the country!!!"

In the freshness of the new Constitution, he would have been booed off the stage, and perhaps tarred and feathered. His party would have been finished.

But today, our major parties fight fiercely over exactly this: to overcome the Separation of Powers and gain control of all three branches of government at once; as if the Separation design were only a game, and overcoming it was the way to win. If either party were to succeed in doing so, they would indeed finally complete their two centuries-long, relentless course of seeking more power. But the price of such "success" would be to finally trash, to defeat, the magnificent design of the American Constitution.

The rest of us might well ask, "Are they insane? What are these people thinking? Have they lost all perspective in the madness of partisanship??"[12]

Party Rage

The Framers witnessed exactly this same force; the spirit of fierce, unyielding competition, from the parties of their time. Only they had their own words for it. They called it **"party rage"**. [*Federalist 9(1)*]

The *Federalist* cites the spectacle of Pennsylvania before the Convention, which

> "...had been for a long time before violently heated and distracted by **THE RAGE OF PARTY**." [*Federalist 50(10)*]

---

[12] In fairness, it should be acknowledged that **extra-constitutional powers** assumed by the Supreme Court have created a crisis and strained our civic life, pulling politics out of normal balance. Politicians, acutely sensitive to where power lies, have been provoked to battle ever more fiercely over the composition of the Court, thinking that their agendas for much of a generation could depend on the outcome of one appointment.
The nature of the Court's usurpation of a power which the **Constitution does not give it**, which has produced a dangerous aneurism in our body politic, will be addressed later. For now, it's enough to note that although the Court's actions have provided an intense *focal point* for **party rage**, the tendency toward that rage already existed; it was not created by the Court. On the other hand, though the parties did not cause this crisis, their response to it has been excessive: degrading, and harmful to the republic. It has been a "**rage**" response of deep division and fierce fighting; featuring character assassinations and terrible slanders—**the stock in trade of the party system**—rather than a response offering remedies, or prospects for healing.

Anti-Party Clause#4

SEPARATED POWERS OF IMPEACHMENT:
TO STOP "PERSECUTIONS" ARISING FROM PARTY RIVALRY

The Framers, who grew up as colonial Englishmen, had a shared knowledge of British history and a familiarity with the Common Law. Among other things, this shared understanding sensitized them to the need for a balance of powers within the national government.

They recognized the necessity for each branch of the government to be able to defend itself against encroachment from the other branches – otherwise, as history showed, encroachments *would* occur, with the result either of a change in the government via takeover (an internal coup, of one branch over another); or a disorder that might only be resolvable through force: civil war. The history of England taught this lesson well.

So the defensive powers of the three Branches were regarded as "core" – essential to the viability of the Constitution.

The President had the power of veto.

Congress was given the power of impeachment over all executive and judicial officers, as well as the ability to discipline its own members.

The Supreme Court had lifetime appointments and non-reducible salaries.[13]

But the Framers divided Congress' power of impeachment between the House and Senate for reasons they explained this way:

> "The division of them between the two branches of the legislature, assigning to one the right of accusing, to the other the right of judging, avoids the inconvenience of making the same persons both accusers and judges; and guards against the **DANGERS OF PERSECUTION, FROM THE PREVALENCY OF A FACTIOUS SPIRIT IN EITHER OF THOSE BRANCHES.**
> [Federalist #66(2)]

Bulkheads and Partitions

Like bulkheads and partitions in a great ship, the Framers built barriers *against* factions, *against* party influences, throughout the structure of the new government they were creating.

But exactly as the Framers had foreseen could happen, when political parties finally did take control of the government, this security-producing power of Impeachment began to be damaged nearly to the point of uselessness by vicious displays of partisanship – an almost inevitable result when virtually all the members of a government are simultaneously members of opposing parties.

---

[13] [but NOT the full power of Review: on August 27, 1787, the Constitutional Convention, in a decision unknown to many historians (and therefore **lost** to the American people), the Convention *denied* to the Supreme Court the role of *"expounding"* (i.e., explaining and interpreting) the Constitution in non-judicial matters.
How the 20th century Court, taking advantage of widespread historical ignorance, threw off restraints observed by past Courts and usurped an *"expounding"* role anyway, in disobedience to the Federal Convention and in complete disregard for the people's conventions held in each state to ratify the Federal Convention's work, will be addressed elsewhere].

Intended as a tool to be used solemnly in the normal course of governing to deter bad conduct or corrupt behavior on the part of individual officeholders without regard to party, the power of impeachment gradually became almost un-useable due to fear of provoking ferocious party-line battles that could tie up the government and divide the country.

By rendering this great Constitutional check on corruption nearly useless, the parties have permitted corrupt conduct in Congress to become commonplace, as long as it is kept below the "radar" of the public's attention. Immoral, occasionally illegal, acts by the Executive branch; and appalling usurpations by the Judiciary, are now virtually immune from correction except through "bad publicity" – a feeble substitute for the prosecution of Law through impeachment.

By rendering this power so nearly useless, the parties have contributed to a lowered respect for the rule of law itself. The full-blown public perception is that high office confers a high degree of immunity upon many who use that office to enrich themselves or to promote private objectives -- their own, or their clients' -- in disregard for the public good.

Hidden corruption is one of the most degrading legacies of the party system.

There will always be corrupt men, in any system; but one of the worst traits of our political parties is their long tradition of providing such people with the opportunity to form nearly impenetrable networks and to hide corruption under a cloak of legitimacy through such things as the awarding of government contracts, jobs, consulting fees, and other lucrative arrangements. They both bring reproach on honest government workers and enable hidden corruption to abound.

Anti-Party Clause #5

SELECTION OF U.S. SENATORS:
AGAINST THE "TAINT OF FACTION"

The Framers originally designed that U S Senators would be selected by the legislatures of the States. Their underlying intention was to formalize the unwritten system of selection they themselves had experienced, and which they had seen yield excellent results.

The process of selection the Framers passed through is crucially important for understanding their entire design of the Constitution; indeed, is crucial for understanding their approach to republican government itself.

We will examine the larger scope of this unwritten system later; but at this juncture we must limit ourselves to one significant point in their reasoning for having state legislatures select U.S. Senators:

The Framers thought the state legislatures would naturally pick the most able, and hopefully the wisest, of their members to be U.S. Senators out of a sense of local pride, patriotism, and civic duty: the prevailing motives they themselves had experienced in pre-partyist America. They expressed their intention that this process would produce a Senate

> "...less apt to be TAINTED BY A SPIRIT OF FACTION.."
> [*Federalist #27(2)*]

"...less apt to be tainted"...This was not a Utopian hope: it was based directly on what the Framers themselves had experienced in a step-by-step process:

Step 1. having earned the respect of their neighbors (in mostly small communities – only Philadelphia and New York had populations over 30,000) by their conduct in life and by honest dealings with neighbors, they were sent to a colonial or state legislature. Then,

Step 2. based on the *respect of peers,* gained during the course of legislative work done together over a period of time, they were chosen by those peers to go to Congress. And, finally

Step 3. based again on earned respect for their work in Congress *and* in their states, some of them were selected as delegates to the Federal Convention.

In short, they had experienced an unwritten filtering system, based at each step on the *earned respect* of fellows and peers, which had yielded the excellent (and reliable) result that men of "Ability and Virtue" (the twin qualifications for prospective officeholders, according to the Framers' worldview) were being advanced to ever more responsible positions.

The fact that this unwritten system of advancement worked so well as to produce the Constitutional Convention is perhaps the only testimony needed to demonstrate its effectiveness. But in fact, this model was effective wherever it prevailed, and formed one of the bedrock assumptions of the Framers on what would make a republic work.

This unwritten system (and its glowing results) provides us a glimpse into the underlying soundness of the culture prevalent in early America. American culture, before the advent of party-ism, strongly adhered to these values: 1.) selection for public office should be based upon *respect earned through honorable conduct in life*; 2.) further advancement should be based on *respect earned through proven ability,* as well as honorable conduct, in office.

But the political expression of that early American culture, i.e., selection for public office based on earned respect in one's community, was about to be weakened and destroyed by the advent of a new and different counter-culture.

America, Weakened and Tainted: The Counter-Culture of Party Strife

This new counter-culture would be laced with accusation and with strife; dominated by ambition and egotism; polluted by vile ideologues, by hypocrisy and by unbridled competition.

American culture itself was about to be debased: infected, weakened and tainted by a partisan mentality.

That mentality was, in fact, a counter-culture, a new *partisan* value system, seeking to replace earlier American values, including the bedrock value of any republic hoping to endure and thrive -- that earned respect (not merely rhetoric or posturing on issues) must be the right road to public office and to advancement.

The Framers' rational, reasonable hope for a "less tainted" Senate was about to be destroyed, along with many other components of early America's clear and sturdy value system, by the new counter-culture of enmity and party strife.

The emerging, *organized* parties did not intend merely to "taint" the Senate; they meant to *take it over* and permanently control it.

Deepening Conflict

Deepening party conflicts during the late 1790's over such issues as the National Bank and the possibility of war with France began to affect social relationships in young America, as the warping effect of the emerging partisan **counter-culture,** fueled and stoked to an intense heat by the epic public battle between Thomas Jefferson and

Alexander Hamilton, took hold. By autumn of 1797, during a crisis with France, the partisan divide in society had reached a point that prompted one observer to write,

> "Men who have been intimate all their lives cross the streets to avoid meeting and turn their heads another way, lest they should be obliged to tip their hats."[14]

Ironically, that observer was none other than Thomas Jefferson, the chief architect and builder of the party system (with the intentional cooperation of James Madison; and the unintended but indispensible contribution of Alexander Hamilton, serving as Jefferson's foil). Jefferson's party successes, which included his strategic alliance with Aaron Burr in the election of 1800, drove the initial development of the party system which would take control of American government, and would triumph over the design of the Framers.

As a partisan spirit took over in the states as well as at the Federal level, the newly dominant parties in state legislatures simply began to pick their most loyal and reliable party members as Senators to represent their party's interests in Washington, along with their states'. Their goal was to control both houses of Congress, thus creating a party-dominated Senate in utter disregard for the Framers' intentions.

Another Casualty

So another of the Framers' carefully thought-out designs was overwhelmed, trampled into uselessness by the seemingly unstoppable energy of the *organized* major parties.

---

[14] Thomas Jefferson to Edward Rutledge, 24 June 1797.

The original method for selecting U.S. Senators was based on the early American value that earned respect from one's peers was the right road to office and to advancement.

But this marvelous gem in the Framers' design, like a raw hundred-carat diamond pulled from the bed of a beautiful river, but never able to be cut and polished; was rendered first useless, and then pernicious by partisanship. It was slimed over and encrusted; its beauty and utility were ruined by ever-increasing party domination of state legislatures and the resulting cronyism.

This marvelous, original selection method, after being ruined, was finally scrapped by the 17th Amendment in favor of direct popular election.

CHAPTER FIVE

The Original Design: an Overview

Elections to the House.
The Veto.
Impeachment Powers.
Selection of U.S. Senators.
The Judicial Branch.

When we 'step back' for an overall look at the Framers' original design, we are immediately struck by the sheer weight, the centrality, of the anti-party clauses and sections listed above. These clauses are not peripheral to the Constitution; they are imbedded in its very core.

The scope and depth of the Framers' antagonism toward the effects of parties is powerfully displayed in these clauses; and in the Framers' comments about them. Their anti-party convictions were not a mere philosophy.

They wrote their convictions about the need for restraining parties into the Constitution (but always in the context of preserving liberty) with the same force and gravity which they employed in providing for other powers: to raise an army, declare war, levy taxes, and perform all acts of government.

The Constitution, in fact, reads like a series of pre-emptive strikes, primarily in the form of structural blocks, in a 'Framers' war' against parties. To portray their profound convictions about the destructive effect of parties as being merely a "philosophical preference" falsifies this history. The Framers meant business.

It was only their commitment to liberty that restrained them from writing provisions much more drastic than those they settled on.

CONCLUSIVE INSIGHT

These clauses, along with the reasoning behind them, provide us a conclusive insight into the Framers' worldview.

Included in the line of reasoning they offered during the ratification process to explain these Constitutional provisions, we find an enlarged list of words being used by the *Federalist* authors to describe the effects of **parties** and **factions** upon a republic:

"pervert"
"divisions"
"diseases"
"contaminate"
"infect"
"pestilential breath"
"demon"
"persecution"

Other examples might be drawn from the *Federalist Papers*, as well as a multitude of citations from various writings and speeches. Since it *was* the Framers' worldview, we find in every part of the Constitution a principled and intelligent *anti*-party conviction underlying the design.

Too Strong?

As was said before, those who may be offended by the phrase "anti-party", thinking it overstated, need only reflect on the list of words above; and ask themselves, "How much more 'anti' could *anyone* have been?"

And they might also ask, "How could historians and party apologists have rationalized their way around the Framers' words? How could even well-intended historians have treated such a powerful subject in a shallow or dismissive way?"

By closing our doors and rolling up our windows against the toxic smog of historical revisionism; and by reading the Framers' original writings for ourselves, we find what seems to us like a new universe of thought. But it only seems new because we didn't know it existed: the Framers' Constitutional worldview *against* political parties.

"..curing the **mischiefs**[15] of faction.."
Federalist #15

James Madison framed the issue in *Federalist #10* this way:

> *"There are two methods of curing the mischiefs of faction: the one, by removing its causes; the other, BY CONTROLLING ITS EFFECTS.*
>
> *There are again two methods of removing the causes of faction: the one, by destroying the liberty which is essential to its existence; the other, by giving to every citizen the same opinions, the same passions, and the same interests.*
>
> *It could never be more truly said than of the first remedy that it was worse than the disease. Liberty is to faction what air is to fire, an aliment [element] without which it instantly expires. But it could not be a less folly to abolish liberty, which is essential to political life, because it nourishes faction than it would be to wish the annihilation of air, which is essential to animal life, because it imparts to fire its destructive agency"*
> *Federalist #10, 3-5*

---

[15] "Mischief" was not a light word in the 1700's, to be used about naughty but cute children; it was a serious word meaning **"destructive ill effects"**, as in "sabotage" or "guerilla warfare".

"…by **controlling its effects**."

We find, throughout the great Document, a determined effort by the Framers, not to destroy parties, but to check them; to contain and neutralize their effects – their potential to degrade and to destroy the life of a republic. They focused not on the *existence* of parties (which they considered inevitable); but on controlling their *effects*; an action they considered essential to the survival and health of the republic.

To Restore

If we are to restore the Framers' original design, we must re-enter their way of thinking. We must use the same tools and values they used, and apply them to our own experience, our history.

We must examine our history as they examined theirs, to find out three things: What has worked; What hasn't – and Why. We have over two hundred years of electoral history to draw lessons from, which they did not have.

We will find that the suffocating effects of party domination over our elections, which has been their means of gaining complete control of our government, can be checked. These suffocating effects can be "controlled" (in the words of *Federalist #10,* above) on behalf of the people, without sacrificing an iota of American liberty.

In fact, the Constitutional *checks* and *balances* we speak of, to be put in place specifically to counter the unjust suffocating dominance by organized parties over our elections, can only be accomplished by EXPANDING liberty, the oxygen of our people and the "air" of our republic.

For the next leg of our journey, we'll assume a familiarity with the general outline of historical events so that we may focus on one objective: the origin of the party system, and the subsequent trashing of key elements in the original Constitutional design.

PART II

CHAPTER SIX

Back To The Fall

From the height of vision and clarity that prevailed in Philadelphia during the summer of 1787, which produced the written Constitution in an atmosphere of vigor, freedom and civility; within four years Thomas Jefferson and Alexander Hamilton began pushing against and testing one another, so absorbed in their rivalry as to be unaware that they were slipping down a wet, muddy slope toward an abyss.

While serving in George Washington's first cabinet, they began to quarrel; their quarreling became progressively more intense. One of the combatants later compared this time in the Cabinet to a daily cockfight.

Thomas Jefferson's self-referencing absolutism, his absolute conviction that his own interpretation of history was not only right, but morally superior to all the men of his time who disagreed with him (i.e., the "Federalists", the network of men who had fought and won the War of Independence; and created the Constitution); combined with a carefully concealed ambition and arrogance, on one hand; but a real hatred of tyranny, and a devotion to republicanism on the other; came face to face with the passion and genius-level abilities of Alexander Hamilton, also unhappily tainted by pride; whose abilities served an even greater ambition.

Like two powerful young eagles, they launched themselves from the slippery slope of their Cabinet confrontations into flight; into their conflicting careers.

Renewing their interrupted fight in mid air, these two eagles locked talons and went into free fall, screaming and tumbling in awful tandem, falling ever deeper into the yawning chasm of conflict and hatred that has so often been the ruin of the human race.

As they dropped, their intense back-and-forth screams, their political diatribes published in highly partisan rival newspapers, pulled ever larger portions of the American people into taking sides. Their fierce conflict, ostensibly over national policies; but with a strong undercurrent of accusation, of sowing suspicion on the motives and characters of one another, had the effect of pulling so much of the citizenry into opposing camps, that it appeared for a while as if it might actually destabilize the new Republic. In certain awful respects, their conflict foreshadowed the coming Civil War.

Undermining

This bitter contest between Jefferson and Hamilton in the 1790's undermined and nearly ruined George Washington's life work.

The first President, revered for fathering America into nationhood and forging the Union, was a unifier; he sought during his entire time as President to create bonds that would knit the States together.

But these two men, and particularly Jefferson, dismissed Washington's efforts at peacemaking between them. They stubbornly advanced their own views, threatening in the process to wrench apart what Washington had labored to build.

BY FAR, THE WORST EFFECT

The vitriol and slander which flew between the camps of Thomas Jefferson and Alexander Hamilton in the late 1790's deepened a sense of crisis and unease plaguing the new republic. Old conflicts and divisions, reaching back to the battle over Ratification and to serious conflicts over relations with Britain and France, were being stirred again.

America had long had disagreeing camps. The rupture with Great Britain and the adoption of a new form of government were occasions of profound disagreement on the part of significant numbers of Americans; disagreement which had only been decided by the outcomes of war and referendum.

Many hoped that the new country might be able to settle, after those epoch- making events, into rhythms of peace and prosperity. But the conflict between Hamilton and Jefferson served to stir up these divided camps anew. Old wounds were re-injured; even as new issues were piled on, creating the sense of a country being pulled apart.

This sense of divided country was bad enough, because it marred the transition period following George Washington's retirement.

Strife As a Permanent Model?

But the worst and most lasting effect of the bitter contest between Alexander Hamilton and Thomas Jefferson (allied with James Madison) was to add new adherents to these latent camps, and cause them to coalesce into **parties**. One side organized sooner; the other later.

Jefferson's side organized first, defeating the loose-knit Federalists in the election of 1800 before they really understood what had hit them. After that election, and for roughly two decades, Jefferson's Democratic-republican government came close to being a one-party system, so thorough were the effects of Jefferson's electoral win, narrow as it was; and the advantage he took of the opportunity to mount a systematic purge of the government, gradually ridding it of almost all Federalists.

When what remained of the shattered and demoralized Federalist camp was at last able to bounce back years later, the two-party system became a fixture in American history.

Saddled

For over two centuries following the election of 1800, America would be increasingly degraded, saddled by the divisiveness and corruption of a **party system**. This history reveals that the bitter, slanderous contest between Thomas Jefferson and Alexander Hamilton (and allies) contained within it the genesis, the actual time of origin, of our two-party system.

Looking back in later years, John Adams lamented something of enormous value he felt the nation had lost in that transformative election of 1800: "We can never have a national President", Adams wrote. "In spite of his own judgment, he must be the President, not to say the tool, of a party."

The Framers' original design – a government "of the people, by the people, and for the people" (in Lincoln's later phrase), in which the people, through their elected representatives, would *rule over all parties,* big and small, making sovereign decisions among their competing claims -- was replaced by a **party system,** in which parties would alternate with one another in control of the government; and thus end up *ruling over the people.*

By simply transforming the people's representatives into their representatives, parties established their seemingly loose, ongoing rule over the people; and overturned the Framers' original design.

Within this party system, party members who held office, with few exceptions, found themselves increasingly ruled by party leaders -- not in terms of their personal freedom, but in terms of what they could accomplish as members of the government.

This is a story so profound in its human elements, so revealing and instructive to all who read or hear it, that it would constitute a tragedy for the human race if this history were to be lost. It merits a more detailed examination.

CHAPTER SEVEN

Conflict

THE SCENE: George Washington's cabinet, in the first Administration under the new Constitution. The unifying power of a shared cause – Independence – has subsided, having been achieved. The second great effort, to write and ratify a new Constitution, is over.

In the dawn of a new order two men, Treasury Secretary Alexander Hamilton and Secretary of State Thomas Jefferson, are finding that they have very different ideas about what role the federal government should play.

Both men are strong-minded. In a turn that deeply concerns the President, their discussions become more heated, their disagreements more frequent and intense. One of the combatants later compares these cabinet meetings to a daily cockfight.

Though their exchanges center on policy issues, it is obvious to the President that a personal conflict has developed, and is headed toward a dangerous level. Worried that their increasingly heated dispute might eventually harm the young country, the great man tries to mediate between the two rivals. But to no avail.

The Undermining Effect

An overlooked historical reality, one underestimated by historians and by party-system apologists, is that both men, by entering into unbridled conflict, undermined George Washington and brought serious and lasting harm to America. They both failed (and one betrayed) the man who fathered the Union into existence and who elevated them to high office.

George Washington, the military commander who won the War of Independence; the first President, the Father of His Country; and the man who presided over the Constitutional Convention, assuring by his enormous strength of presence the civility and endurance needed for its work (these descriptions were merited almost unanimously in the minds of his countrymen) – this man had dedicated most of his adult life to not only bringing forth, but to unifying, the new country.

But in stark contrast, the fierce rivalry between Thomas Jefferson and Alexander Hamilton was rooted not only in differing philosophies and backgrounds, but in personal enmity and ego; leading both of them to reject George Washington's sound judgment that the issues they fought over so bitterly were in reality "not irreconcilable".

"…not irreconcilable"

Failed historians, by stepping into the exact outlines of Jefferson and Hamilton's footprints – uncritically recording their partisan arguments – have ended up acting as party-system apologists by avoiding this perfectly sound judgment from George Washington, choosing instead to glorify the drama of early party conflict.

This failure has left us, as modern-day citizens, with the task of sorting out the history for ourselves, simply to find out what really happened.

Hamilton and Jefferson's bitter struggle led them both to undermine the first President's lifetime work. Both of them, but especially Jefferson, [*"especially"*, because Hamilton's fighting came more as an instinctive reaction against Jefferson's ominous approach of deliberately "stirring hostility to the government", as John Marshall, the Great Chief Justice, evaluated it].

But whether from a faction-producing offensive strategy; or as a fierce defense of the newborn government; both men ended up willing to inflame divisions and to split the country into what John Adams said he dreaded most: two great permanent camps constantly warring with one another.

This result (the party system) which in the beginning was only one of a number of possible outcomes for the new republic, was abhorrent to Washington, to Adams, to John Marshall and to many other Federalist patriots who had led the movement for, and won, Independence.

What historians have generally failed to explore is the reality behind George Washington's sound judgment: that much of the conflict between the two men was unnecessary. Jefferson's and Hamilton's positions on many issues could have been reconciled; with enough time, good will and mutual respect; if the men were willing. But they were not.

History-Changing Paradigm

The implications of George Washington's sound judgment are staggering; and would certainly re-write most of our history books if historians were to listen to it and take note.

The terrible divisions left from the conflicts of the late 1790's, when old wounds were deepened and fresh ones created, were **not** inevitable. On the contrary, the issues fought over were intensified, magnified, and some *manufactured* by what Washington labeled the "rank spirit" of party.

With the exception of slavery, most of the issues involved in that first toxic dump into the national psyche of vicious partisan attacks could have been negotiated and compromised.

But historians have generally taken the easy route.

The eminent standings of James Madison, Alexander Hamilton, and Thomas Jefferson have made it easy to conclude that the advent of partisanship, and therefore the development of political parties, must have been inevitable. If *these* men fell into partisanship, the reasoning goes, then it must have been unavoidable. Lesser men might have made things even worse.

So far, this reasoning is correct. It is true that parties are inevitable, given human nature. And there will always be a Jefferson or a Hamilton; a Hitler or a Lenin; or a Kennedy or a Bush, to lead them.

A Failure Of Thinking

But at that point, this line of reasoning fails.

Parties are indeed inevitable. They will have leaders.

But to take the next step and assume that therefore the *takeover of our national and state governments by parties must also have been inevitable,* is wrong, is unfounded. Such a huge, wrong leap is an assumption that must come either from intellectual laziness or from the mental conditioning created in the minds of many historians simply by dint of growing up under the party system.

It is not true that a party takeover of the government was unavoidable. The Framers' viewpoint, in fact, was exactly the opposite. They expected parties to form; but did not expect them to take over.

That happened because the parties figured out very quickly how to dominate our unprotected, unstructured (i.e., un-checked and un-balanced) elections; it did not happen simply because parties formed.

And historically, Jefferson, Madison and Hamilton could have had the unbridled party-forming effect they did only because George Washington was gone, was out of their way.

Gone

Modern Americans might gain some insight into this by reflecting on the Civil Rights movement. When Martin Luther King was killed, the movement went on; and some notable personalities did their best to lead it, to fill King's shoes. These were generally well motivated and intelligent people; but they simply lacked the element of greatness many Americans had experienced, then missed, in King.

In a much greater context, because it concerned the founding of the nation itself, when George Washington left the scene, no one could replace him. The rare elements of true greatness; and his gift of sound judgment; were gone.

What is difficult to convey, with so much time intervening, is how much the country missed him. Both Hamilton and Jefferson were eminent and accomplished; but they simply were far lesser men.

2 Fathers and ...

George Washington was the father of his country, America.

But Thomas Jefferson was the father of a faction, a deep division **in** America, who conducted a botched and embittering amputation of much of the founding American leadership, (i.e., the Federalists.)

And Alexander Hamilton simply led his party too passionately.

In the decades after Washington and Adams, the weakness of the party system -- its inherent tendency to promote animosities and disagreements, not to heal them -- fed into the monstrous currents leading toward Civil War.

Great Issues, Great Egos

The conflict between Alexander Hamilton and Thomas Jefferson had more serious implications than normal political conflicts precisely because each of them was such a plausible -- and capable -- representative of his region and background.

The cultures of their two regions were markedly different, and contained vastly different interests.

But neither personal conflict nor political division were inevitable results of these regional differences. George Washington was a living example and a powerful political force toward the opposite: national unity.

THE TWO EAGLES

Thomas Jefferson - Virginia landholder and philosopher, agrarian, Democratic republican party founder & leader, slave owner.

VS.

Alexander Hamilton - Abolitionist, soldier, aide to Washington, financial genius, Federalist party leader, New York lawyer.

Context

Enormous differences between North and South would likely have caused the emergence of *some* form of major parties within the new country, regardless of individual personalities. But personalities also shape history, and give it the precise form it eventually takes. And so it was in the conflict that developed between these two men, Thomas Jefferson and Alexander Hamilton; in which we find not merely a catalyst for competing regional forces, but the actual formation, the genesis, of the two-party system that took root and took over in America.

The fascination of history lies in the people who lived it and made it. The study of those people inevitably involves an attempt to understand what they were thinking, and their motives for doing what they did. This is not an easy exercise; but it is one that must be undertaken. It can only legitimately be based on convincing evidence from that person's own words and patterns of behavior.

One advantage of this kind of looking back is that we often have a more complete and accurate picture of the other people involved in an historical setting than any particular historical actor could have had at that time.

It is therefore revealing to compare what one historical figure *thought* and *said* about another (or about a series of events), against what historians can reliably show to have been the actual case; in order to evaluate how close to reality the judgments and opinions of that first historical figure may (or may not) have been.

This is an invaluable tool for historians. In our case, it's also a crucial exercise for understanding the genesis and the "DNA" of American political parties.

EAGLE ONE:
The Virginia Mentality

Understanding Thomas Jefferson's thought process has challenged historians for two centuries. Part of the understanding they've sought lies in certain little-known realities in the history of Virginia and the South.

In the 18th century culture of Virginia, a sort of mythic value held sway, which eventually led Virginians, and much of the South, to consider that their way of life rivaled the ancient civilizations of Athens and Rome – both of which included slavery – for having arrived at the very pinnacle of civilized human development.

So many American successes had been led by Virginians and Carolinians, that it is understandable how Southern culture could unconsciously start to take too much credit for being the real "source", or wellspring, of America itself. In this parochial way of thinking, America was more or less "Virginia, writ large", in the brilliant, summary phrase popularized by Edmond Morgan.

Virginians, and Southerners in general, were not walking around in shame, with their heads down, over slavery. On the contrary, most were protective and proud of their culture; glad to point out elements of courtesy and hospitality in it, which they long felt were sorely lacking in the 'crass and commercial' North.

In Southern slaveholding culture, certain values prevailed and their attendant costs were accepted. These values included parameters for what made a "good" owner or master of slaves, versus a "bad" one. A "bad" master was one who was unnecessarily arbitrary or cruel. A "good" master was supposed to be just, to demonstrate decent treatment and care toward his slaves, even while maintaining absolute control over them. Contrary to modern stereotypes, there were more than a few households where genuine affection existed between slaves and owners.

But even in such "benign" situations, the *costs* of slavery were also accepted. These costs included the non-negotiable, unquestionable need to maintain complete control by whites, especially owners; and complete submission on the part of all slaves. Thus an owner who became too lenient or familiar with his slaves out of human kindness might face open criticism and rebuke from his neighbors, especially if any of his slaves somehow "bothered" or irritated white people.

So the accepted costs of slavery included the use of whippings, chains, and occasionally hanging, for recalcitrant or rebellious slaves. Subjugation was the *sine qua non* of slaveholding culture, which had to be enforced by the whole of the society.

Abolitionist vs. Slave Owner

As if to add a final element of danger to their bitter struggle, and in an ominous foreshadowing of future national disaster, Thomas Jefferson led a committee in the Virginia legislature to re-write that state's slave codes; but Alexander Hamilton helped found the Manumission Society to protect freed slaves in New York

Jefferson proposed some of the most severe measures heard of up to that time, including a provision that any freed slave, or any white woman who had a child with a black man, had to leave Virginia within one year or be declared "outside the protection of the laws". This would have made such persons vulnerable to lynching, re-enslavement, beating, looting, gang-rape or other mob actions.

There seems not to have been any particular indication of personal malice on Jefferson's part in this. He valued Reason over human customs or traditions; and exalted his own reason over any religion or Scripture. (He referred privately to the Bible as a "dunghill"[16], in letters he instructed the recipients to keep secret, from which he had, through the use of Reason, been able to extract a few diamonds. These diamonds he thought he found among the sayings of Jesus; whom he regarded as a great moral teacher; but as human, not divine – a viewpoint he also instructed his correspondents to keep secret.)

But Jefferson's Reason had convinced him that the Black and White races could not co-exist peaceably "under the same government" (i.e., if blacks were free).

So he probably saw such drastic, heartless measures as the ones he proposed for the Virginia slave code as simply necessary in order to prevent the buildup of a 'mixed polity' in Virginia.

But quite apart from any question of personal malice, there is a deeper sort of *impersonal* malice which results from ideology or dogma being carried to its logical conclusion in law without the tempering effects of human kindness; or of wisdom.

Since the proposed statute would have made Virginia a virtual state of terror for the individuals affected by it, it is only fair that Mr. Jefferson (or any other ideologue) be held morally accountable for the *effects* of their proposals (and laws), not just for the logic or the 'Reason' in them.

The Abolitionist

Alexander Hamilton was instinctively a fighter, a trait which more than once went too far and marred his life. But when applied in a good cause, this trait could have admirable effect. Hamilton was arguably the most ardent and active Abolitionist among all the

[16] Thomas Jefferson to John Adams, 1813; quoted in Hutson, *The Founders on Religion*, 30.

Founders. He helped to start and lead the New York Manumission Society. The Society was formed as an alarmed reaction to the kidnapping of freed slaves off the streets of New York by "bounty-hunter" agents of Southern slavers.

The Slave Owner

Thomas Jefferson, though plagued by the contradiction of slavery to his own noble words in the Declaration of Independence, "... that all men are created equal," seemed able to rationalize that contradiction largely through sheer racism.

He once wrote a monogram detailing the inferiority of the Negro race to whites in terms of lower intellect; of body odor; and, in Jefferson's mind, their lack of musical sensibilities.

He thus became a philosophical enabler – in spite of publicly deploring the slave trade and musing on ways that slavery might eventually be phased out -- for the maintaining of slavery already in place and (not incidentally) of his own style of living. Jefferson felt called during his entire life to defend Virginia and the South.

The "Southern Strategy"

In one letter to his fellow Virginian James Madison, Jefferson was outlining their political strategy, one which would strengthen "the Southern cause". Upon reflection, he crossed out the word, "Southern", and wrote "republican" above it, in apparent realization that his political *strategy* had to be national, even if his heart belonged to Virginia and the South.

When it came time late in life to design the inscription for his tombstone, Jefferson listed on it his authorship of the Declaration of Independence; his passage of Virginia's statute on Religious Liberty, and his founding of the University of Virginia.

Pointedly left off his tombstone was any reference to having served two terms as President of the United States. When Jefferson referred to "my country", he meant Virginia, not America; a usage which seems odd today, but was not entirely uncommon at the time: Madison, for one, did the same.

Protecting Virginia and the Southern way of life was a sincerely held value for both Madison and Jefferson at a time when the preponderance of power, numerically and economically, was shifting North.

In spite of Jefferson's Virginia-centric mindset, and the fact that a majority of Americans voted against him in the election of 1800 [he won because 3/5ths of the "votes" of Negro slaves in the Southern states counted for him[17]; enough to throw the election into the House of Representatives] he was nevertheless convinced that he represented about 95% of Americans as far as the true meaning of the American Revolution was concerned. For Jefferson and many other Southerners, the *true* essence of America was "Virginia, writ large"; and republicanism.

Land vs. Money

An essential part of the Virginia mentality equated land with wealth. If a man owned land, and had slaves to work it, he was wealthy; even if he was cash poor.

Using credit – borrowing – to provide cash flow from harvest to harvest was an unpleasant necessity on the one hand, for a majority of planters; but it was also a perk, a natural result of holding the

---

[17] For purposes of representation and taxation, the Constitutional Convention settled on a compromise: each slave would count as 3/5 of a citizen. This meant paying lower taxes on the part of slave states; but it also meant fewer representatives in Congress. Slave votes were not taken or counted; they were simply awarded or bundled in with white votes, according to each state's allotment of presidential electors.

true wealth, land. Using credit became a way of life for many
Virginia planters, including Thomas Jefferson and James Madison.

Overdoing the use of credit was an easy trap to fall into, for those
who thought of themselves as innately wealthy. Many planters
became inextricably trapped in a cycle of borrowing and debt, most
of it owed to English bankers and commercial traders.

One major exception to this debilitating trend was George
Washington, one of the few Virginia planters with the foresight and
business sense to diversify out of tobacco into wheat and other cash
crops, thus protecting his family's finances from the ups and downs
of the tobacco market and its attendant debt cycle.[18]

In Contrast

Thomas Jefferson, on the other hand, was so deeply in debt that
he lamented at one point that it had become impossible for him
to enjoy life anymore. Both Jefferson and Madison ended up
bankrupt.

For Jefferson, the forced sale of Monticello in his old age, with
everything in it and nearly all his slaves (except his children by
Sally Hemmings; but evidently not excepting Hemmings herself),
provided a tragic and sordid ending to his career.

But up to that point, he had lived like a multi-millionaire, enjoying
fine wine, art and expensive furniture; and constantly improving
Monticello. Even after selling all he owned, Jefferson's creditors lost
an estimated two to five million dollars in today's currency.

It is no surprise, then, that Jefferson loathed the banking industry
and hated bankers, especially English bankers. For him, banking
and finance were means by which clever men brought other men

---

[18]   Ellis, *His Excellency George Washington*, 52, 53.

into subjugation and misery, ruining their lives by threatening to take all they owned.

There seems to have developed a connection in Jefferson's mind between what he saw as the distant and uncaring, arbitrary and selfish power – i.e., tyranny -- exercised by kings over their subjects; and the distant, uncaring, selfish tyranny of bankers over the people they had brought into financial subjugation.

"Monarchists" and "monocrats" (referring to an elite, an aristocracy that included financiers, always presumed to exploit common people) were two of the names Jefferson used most often to describe those he saw as enemies of the Revolution, and of the common people.

Money vs. Land

Alexander Hamilton, born a bastard in poverty on a Caribbean island but put in charge of a commercial shipping company at the age of 14 because of his extraordinary abilities, (and because of his perceived good character and mental toughness); for Hamilton, in drastic contrast to Jefferson, mastering finance and commerce was his instrument of liberation, the open road to great accomplishment.

CONFLICT OVER BANKING

Jefferson and Madison vehemently opposed Hamilton's proposal for a National Bank. Their opposition became a central "plank" in the Democratic-republican platform.

But one reality is inescapable to the modern mind, and cannot be avoided: Thomas Jefferson did not understand banking; nor the world of finance. The man who divided America over the National Bank did not understand that which he hated and opposed.

Wrong, But Right?

And yet, as is often the case with Jefferson, he also put his finger on the crucial danger of banking, observing that if the power to *create money* were put into the hands of any group of men, there would be an almost inevitable danger of that power being abused.

"MONARCHISTS"

Thomas Jefferson was convinced that many leading Federalists were "monarchists". His characterization of Hamilton was that he "was not only a monarchist, but for a monarchy bottomed on corruption". Jefferson never gave this idea up; in fact this accusation, as false as it was, formed one of the core tenets of the party Jefferson was drawing together, at first called the Democratic-republicans, then just "republicans".
(Not to be confused with the modern-day Republican Party.)

Jefferson's own words and, later, his unwarranted and unfounded accusation (leveled anonymously through allies in Congress) against Hamilton, accusing him of fraud at the Treasury, make it seem entirely plausible that he may have been at least partially motivated by feeling, more than once, the stinging embarrassment of defeat in his face-to-face encounters with Hamilton during their time in the cabinet, which Jefferson later called a time of "martyrdom" for him.

Jefferson warned James Madison in a letter that Hamilton was a formidable foe, a "colossus" astride his party, and "a host within himself".

Hamilton was brilliant in debate, the owner of a quick mind embedded in an ultra-confident personality, who was capable of immediate confrontation; while Jefferson, no less strong in his opinions, was nevertheless more reserved in personality; with a slower, more philosophical thought process.

It would have been galling for a man like Jefferson to appear to lose in face-to-face debate to a "quicker" or "more clever" man.

Such apparent defeat would have been more galling to Jefferson than to most men. Jefferson's overarching characteristic, during his entire career, consisted in a sort of absolutism, an unshakable conviction that his own thoughts and opinions (which he considered the products of Reason, guided by his innate moral sense) were right.

When applied in a good cause, this absolutist trait produced some of the most soaring prose of all time: the wording of the Declaration of Independence. His service in that document was to put into writing the thoughts which were shared by almost all the men present in Congress at that time; in that sense, not much of its substance was original.

But Jefferson's prose was so sublimely powerful in expressing their common view that it earned him an enduring place in American history; much to John Adams' surprise, who thought of the Declaration as a product of *his* committee in Congress, with Jefferson simply acting as a draftsman.

Absolutely Convinced

But on the downside, this trait of Jefferson's also included the absolute conviction that his own understanding of the American Revolution was superior to that of virtually every other leading member of the Founding generation. This thought was delusional on its face, and dismissive of the ideas and experiences of others. It seems astounding—almost unbelievable--in its arrogance, until one gains some grasp of Jefferson's private belief system.

But he was so convinced of this misbegotten conviction that he determined to use whatever means he could find to *rout from the new government* all the Founders who disagreed with him (i.e., the "Federalists"), despite the fact that they were the men who had led the movement that became the Revolution; had fought and won the War of Independence; and had created the American Constitution.

Despite the record of these men called Federalists, Jefferson was convinced that he had a truer understanding of the *republican* nature of the Revolution than they did; he was also convinced that the majority – about 95%, by his estimate -- of Americans agreed with him.

"I will bury Federalism," he wrote to James Madison, "into an abyss from which it will never emerge."

Jefferson was in many ways an early ideologue. His time of service in France had confirmed in him a deep hatred toward tyranny, which meant tyrants: aristocrats and kings.

The corruption and decadence he witnessed in the French ruling classes; and the abjectness of the common people verified, in his mind, this part of his worldview.

Jefferson's core belief was that human beings were basically good; and the presence of **evil** in the world was due to the ruling classes' abuse of their superior strength to subjugate the common people and misrule them for their own benefit.

EVIL, in Jefferson's thinking, was *produced* by tyrants, by kings and aristocrats; by "priests" (and bankers). Get rid of them, and the innate goodness of men would be free to manifest. The presence of any "privileged" class, whether the result of money or birth, offended his sense of republicanism; and he was determined to prove that the overwhelming majority of Americans agreed.

Jefferson's private belief system, assigning the presence of evil in the world to abusive conduct by rulers and ruling classes, made him capable of arriving at extreme, occasionally very dangerous conclusions, as historian Joseph Ellis relates.

When the National Bank was established by vote of Congress, for example, Jefferson communicated to James Madison his opinion that it might constitute treason for a citizen of a state – they were both Virginians -- to accept the decision of the federal government (which he likened to a *foreign government)* in matters that should be the sole jurisdiction of the states; (i.e., "treason" against Virginia, in their case).

The two men kept this communication secret; after this time, they wrote to one another in a code known only to themselves.

This same self-generated belief system led to Jefferson's seemingly inexplicable hatred for Federalism and all things Federalist. Though perfectly capable of acknowledging their contributions and their qualities as human beings, he nevertheless saw the Federalists as the (probably unwitting) servants of an ancient evil order of things, dominated by "kings and priests", and aristocrats; an order which he was determined to destroy by thoroughly establishing republicanism.

Jefferson, in his private comments about Jesus Christ (whom he considered human, not divine) seemed to identify with what Jefferson interpreted as Jesus' mission, which he thought was to overthrow corrupt authorities misruling the Jewish religion.

Jefferson seems to have concluded that Jesus had some similarity, in that regard, to himself.

PARTY SPIRIT

Once any man reaches the point of identifying his opponents as somehow representative of evil, rather than fellow human beings with a different viewpoint, then it becomes very difficult for others to understand that man's motives. Equally difficult, is to guess "how far will he go?"

Alexander Hamilton, with his fierce defense of the new government, seemed to trigger the pent-up hatred in Jefferson for all things "evil" or unjust which he included in the word "monarchist".

Jefferson, like most men with a self-invented belief system, was blind to the fact that his thought system was based upon an assumption about himself as being good, the man of Reason, able to judge all human history.

But what did *that* assumption on Jefferson's part make of those who disagreed with him, his opponents?

Especially those like Chief Justice John Marshall, who did not at all buy into his cousin Tom Jefferson's self-ordained "marvelous good guy, judge-of-all-humanity" status, but instead evaluated Jefferson's actions by a more traditional standard: right and wrong. By that standard, he despised Jefferson and, it is fair to say, hated his actions and his effect on America.

The assumption of one's own goodness, and therefore the sheer *wrongness* of one's opponents, is the hidden ground men often use to justify evil decisions or amoral acts; or lying.

PARTY 'DNA'

This element of self-delusion about one's own goodness is an essential part of "party spirit", which the Framers warned so strongly against; it is buried deeply—embedded--in party DNA.

Without understanding this element, it would be impossible to understand the history of parties and partisanship in America.

Because Thomas Jefferson was our first **party**-system founder and leader, we should closely study his conduct and its effect on this formative period of American politics.

The Mazzei Letter

Jefferson's hidden belief system caused occasional blunders which set back his political plans. At one point, he wrote a letter to Philipe Mazzei, an Italian friend, that referred to the "despotic" regime of George Washington and the Federalists. Mazzei promptly leaked the letter, causing a scandal that Jefferson couldn't make "go away".

Who's a Despot?

Quite apart from any "political scandal" consequence, the real interest of this letter lies in Jefferson's expressed thoughts. George Washington, linked to despotism?

Objectively, such a characterization bordered on absurdity. Washington operated on a code of honor; which entailed respect for others. Keeping Jefferson in his cabinet, who strongly disagreed with him on a number of issues, was a clear indication of Washington's governing style, which respected the integrity of other men. The same was true of John Adams.

Jefferson's later governing style as President, on the other hand, turned out to look quite a bit more "despotic" than either of his predecessors. As the first party boss, he kept his party members in line to a much greater extent than either Washington or Adams would ever have dreamed of doing – it was simply not in their worldview.

Jefferson's party members, especially legislators, had far less room to think for themselves than officeholders in the Washington or Adams administrations.

The "ideologue" side of Jefferson, his absolute conviction that he was right, must have made it seem natural to him that his thoughts should prevail over those of others, especially in his own party.

Without at least a partial grasp of Jefferson's beliefs, it would be impossible to make any sense of his statement in the Mazzei letter: it was simply not based on reality; but upon an invisible link inside Jefferson's head, a link to his core beliefs about the source of the world's evils being tyrannical rulers and bad (non-republican) governmental systems.

Esoteric

Jefferson's more esoteric enthusiasms, several of them brilliantly searched out by E.M. Halliday[19], included an epic poem supposedly written by a Homer-like figure from antiquity named Ossian. It told about the legendary doings of a pre-historic, mythical tribe which once lived in the forests of northern Europe. Jefferson memorized long passages of this poem, which he could recite verbatim in the company of fellow enthusiasts.

The very existence of an Ossian was controversial; a consensus eventually developed that Ossian was invented by a poetic Scottish writer named Macpherson.

---

[19] Halliday, *Understanding Thomas Jefferson*.

The intriguing question arises: what appeal did the pseudo-epic poem have for Jefferson?

Because the poem was set in prehistory, and was highly romanticized. it would have been possible for its readers to believe that such a people-group may actually have existed. And if they existed in prehistory as the poem described, it would seem likely they lived quite well, even heroically, together; without need of highly complex or formal government.

Such a myth would have had obvious parallels with the "Noble Savage" concept which swept through European intellectual circles for a time; and which romanticized American Indians in similar terms. (Sadly, it was mostly an invention of the Europeans; and tended to trivialize the realities and accomplishments—including their portion of genuine nobility--of Native American lives. Reducing them to a sort of fad status described in European terms among cultural elites.)

But the appeal of this Ossian legend to Jefferson (we can speculate) could have lain in its support for the idea that human nature was basically good; that the potential existed for men to live together without need for complicated government; and that the major evils in the world were mainly the product of bad rulers, and bad (un-republican) systems of government.

U.Va

Later in life, these beliefs led Jefferson to design the University of Virginia along lines very similar to "experimental" or "alternative" colleges set up in the 1960's; featuring great freedom for students; few requirements; easy familiarity with faculty, and much leeway in choice of subjects for study, etc.

In theory, it sounded promising; idyllic for scholars.

This plan for U.Va might offer insights into Jefferson's character; among which would be that Jefferson himself was the sort of student who would have thrived in such an atmosphere: self-motivated and eager to learn.

On the other hand, it would also indicate that his understanding of human nature was woefully inadequate.

Within a few months, some of the first group of students fell into drinking and partying. Then they rioted and ended up destroying a considerable amount of property. The subsequent public investigation was nothing short of mortifying for Jefferson.

UNDERPINNINGS

John Adams, along with many other Federalists, considered all men capable of producing either evil **or** good. The Federalists thought that the Constitution needed to protect the rights of a minority precisely because an aroused majority would be perfectly capable of wrongly trampling the minority's rights; which, if it happened, would express of a sort of civic evil.

Jefferson's worldview, which rejected the traditional Christian teaching prevalent in the culture around him, [that all men are capable of making either good or evil choices; choices for which they will one day give an account to God, who will judge them] in favor of the utopian view that human nature is intrinsically good--left him with no viable explanation for the presence of evil in the world except to find some group, or social stratum, to blame it on. Philosophically, he was trapped by his own assumptions.

These assumptions, or products of his Reason, frequently shared by later "class warfare" ideologues, caused him to continue supporting the leaders of the French Revolution long after they instituted the Terror; a time when cut-off heads were rolling into the gutters of

Paris. This led to his famous "Adam and Eve" letter, in which he defended the slaughter in France to his friend, William Short.

The "Adam And Eve" Letter

"Rather than it [the French Revolution] should have failed," Jefferson wrote, "I would have seen half the earth desolated. Were there but an Adam and an Eve left in every country, and left free, it would be better than it now is."[20]

"Half the earth desolated." "…left in every country,…and left free." Jefferson's dramatic flair with words, his ability to fashion amazingly powerful prose, still thrills intellectual fools to this day. They willingly look past the content of his words, and assume that "he didn't really mean that".

But Thomas Jefferson, if capable of anything, was capable of saying what he meant. He *said* that it was worth it to him to have *tens of millions* of corpses lying about; entire populations killed and countries desolated, if only two people in each country were left "free", by his definition.

The word "extreme" is not extreme enough to describe how heartless and irresponsible, [how "Utopian", in 18th century debate terms], or just immature, such a way of thinking was, and is. It was an early example of the reality that "ideas have consequences": a reality which the human race would witness on a horrifying scale in the twentieth century.

If these "Adam and Eve" lines had been written by a modern college student, a decent instructor would probably write next to them, "Grow up."

---

[20] Thomas Jefferson to William Short, 3 January 1793.

James Madison found he had to do something like that when Jefferson announced to him in a letter his most recent epiphany: that the U.S. Constitution should be re-written every nineteen years, on the principle that no generation had a right to bind another into its chosen form of government.

Madison was able to convince his misguided friend to keep this heady, unreal theory on a shelf; and not let it get out in public.

THE DEEPENING DIVIDE

Most Federalists, on the other hand, were appalled at the slaughter in France.

And they tended to believe, whether they had seen this particular letter or not, that Jefferson meant what he said; and he said much in support of the French Revolution.

A Brutal Start

In outward results, Jefferson was the loser during his time in the Cabinet. Both the President and Congress backed Alexander Hamilton's fiscal program, among other contested issues. In the vulgar but accurate speech of modern political operatives, Jefferson repeatedly got his political butt kicked by Alexander Hamilton during their time in the cabinet; an experience he did not relish.

But if Jefferson lost in face-to-face debates and his views lost out in Washington's policy judgments, these things did not change his deeply held convictions. Instead, they had the effect of energizing him. He left the immediate scene of struggle and began to draw together a network, starting with James Madison, which would become the first American political party.

"Proof of Insanity"

Just before leaving the cabinet, Jefferson expressed his (by this time) nearly paranoid conviction, in a vehement outburst to George Washington, that Hamilton was "secretly a monarchist" and that his fiscal program was designed "to prepare a change from the present republican form of government to that of a monarchy."[21]

The President, taken aback, rejected the accusation. Washington knew his long-time aide well. Though he and Hamilton "both favored a strong executive", Washington said, neither Hamilton nor anyone else in his administration wanted to "restore monarchy". Anyone *thinking* such a thing, the offended President went on to say, thereby offered "proof of their insanity!"[22]

Though normally courteous, George Washington's angered, powerful rebuke made his position impossible for Jefferson to misconstrue.

What Jefferson should not have been unaware of was the insult to Washington contained in his accusation. If Hamilton was a secret "monarchist", then who was he secretly planning to make king? Himself, or Washington? Either answer would have been not only completely wrong, but also an insult to the man who had given his life to father the Republic into existence.

But hearing truth spoken – that there were no "monarchists" in the government – and getting a face-to-face rebuke from the most respected man in the country (perhaps, by this time, in the world) did not deter Thomas Jefferson, who remained absolutely convinced of his conclusions. He departed the cabinet, and affected a retirement to his plantation in Virginia.

---

[21] Thomas Jefferson to George Washington, 23 May 1792.
[22] Ellis, *American Creation*, 184. Quoting from Record of Conversation with President Washington, 6 August 1783.

Looking back, we can see in this vignette a near-perfect illustration of how men's personality characteristics do not merely "affect" the course of history; but quite often determine it.

George Washington's sound judgment, heated and tempered on the anvil of events, of necessary decisions made as lives hung in the balance and the destiny of a nation was decided told him—easily, quickly—that the men who served with him in a long, grueling war to establish independence from a monarch; and who now served with him in governing the new constitutional Republic they'd risked their lives for; that none of them wanted to "restore monarchy".

To think otherwise must have seemed stupidly perverse to the President; or contrived, especially from a man who did not serve in the army.

But the man in front of Washington DID think that way—that the new government harbored many "secret monarchists".

What informed this man so was his self-referencing absolutism, which caused him to interpret even casual dinner conversation about the relative strengths and weaknesses of different forms of government strictly in terms of his own ideological beliefs.

Like a dedicated communist of today, who *hates* capitalism in any form, Thomas Jefferson *hated* monarchy; and could not tolerate even a casual conversation which failed to denounce it; or mentioned any possible merit to it.

This singular personality trait in Jefferson, that of the ideologue valuing his own thoughts far above others', would go on to undermine Washington's life work of unifying America; and would eventually lodge a permanent quarrel <u>into</u> America in the form of the **party** system.

Jefferson had been away in France during the entire time of the Constitution's writing and ratification. Many genuine patriots, especially in the South, had opposed the new Constitution, fearful among other things of too strong a central government.

These "anti-federalists" included many acquaintances of both Jefferson and James Madison. In spite of his friendship with Madison, who was one of the main architects of the Constitutional design, Jefferson also opposed the stronger central government he found in place on his return from France, and persuaded his fellow Virginian to work with him for a more "republican" (and pro-South) interpretation of the document.

Jefferson's worldview enabled him to correctly identify a powerful undercurrent in post-Revolutionary America. His hatred of aristocracy resonated well with a widespread resentment in the new republic for any remnant of a "class" structure in society. The new Constitution forever banned any establishment of hereditary titles; but Jefferson shrewdly discerned a deeper current of popular resentment, often called the "leveling spirit" by 18th century writers, against any privileges bestowed by birth or by money.

The irony was that Jefferson himself was highly privileged. He inherited large holdings of land and slaves and lived like a multi-millionaire, enjoying fine wine, art, and furniture; while constantly remodeling an exquisite mansion of his own design.

Plain Dress

But Jefferson dressed very plainly, in order to identify with "republican" citizens; as against the privileged "elite".

This lifestyle contradiction was possibly a minor factor in Alexander Hamilton's assessment of Jefferson as a hypocrite, but a far greater factor would have been his protection for and maintenance of slavery; which Hamilton vigorously opposed.

Historians have identified a number of contradictions and puzzles in Jefferson's makeup. He's been called "the American Sphinx" and "the most dangerous man in America", among other things. But in adding up the sum total of his life and writings, few have concluded that he was entirely cynical, or merely pretending to hold popular positions. On the contrary, wrong or right, he seems to have absolutely believed his convictions.

FOUNDER AND LEADER

But Jefferson was more than a thinker; he was a masterful politician, the founder and leader of the first organized faction, the first political party, in America.

In looking back at political careers in the 1700's, one thing for the modern person to remember is that there were no professional "PR" men around in the 1700's; no "image crafters".

But canny politicians and public figures nevertheless instinctively grasped the importance of "managing" their public image, their reputation. With no cameras or "photo-ops" around, real-life occasions had to be used to project an image.

So it is, as historian Joseph Ellis relates, that we would find a young Benjamin Franklin puffing and wrestling heavy wheelbarrows full of printer's supplies through the streets of Philadelphia at exactly the times of day he knew he would be noticed by other businessmen. It was a deliberate tactic by Franklin: "PR", 18th century style.

So for Jefferson to dress plainly in public was more likely an honest statement of his republican sentiments, in spite of his very rich private lifestyle, than it was mere cynicism or hypocrisy.

In drawing together America's first political party, Jefferson tapped into widespread resentment against privilege and hammered relentlessly at the commonly voiced Federalist sentiment that the "better" part of society (themselves) should be in charge of the government.

In hindsight, it is easy to see that this particular aspect of Federalism as a political philosophy was doomed. The election of 1800 more than likely turned on this issue, whether or not it was fairly argued. Susan Dunn, among many others, rightly concludes that the results of this election permanently doomed social elitism as a defensible position in American politics.

Jefferson, for good or ill the master of powerful prose (though a very poor public speaker), was canny enough to focus his animosity on Alexander Hamilton. His true direction was in opposition to all Federalists, which included George Washington, John Adams, and a long list of war heroes and patriots.

Washington, already being called the Father of His Country, was beloved and honored; so he seemed untouchable.

Hamilton, who offended many, was not.

Jefferson calculated with unsentimental shrewdness in a letter to James Madison that George Washington would soon be out of their way.

Secret Payments
And a Poisoned Atmosphere

Jefferson for some time secretly paid a journalist named James Callendar who attacked Hamilton in his Philadelphia newspaper, the *Aurora*. Around the time Jefferson left the cabinet, insinuations about George Washington also began to increase in the paper, sly hints that he was not as honest as people thought; and had almost lost the War. It was said in the paper that he might actually have been *a traitor*, a secret agent for the British. And that he was getting senile, was no longer fit for the Presidency.

These slanders were spread like poisoned bait for a purpose: to destroy Federalism, and Federalists, by defiling the love and respect held in public sentiment for the most prominent Federalist of all (even though George Washington himself was still trying to maintain neutrality in the face of growing party venom).

This tactic, or willingness, to destroy the affections in people's minds and hearts through character assassination and through malicious innuendo in order to win political power was encoded in party DNA very early in our history. It has only gotten worse over time, and is perhaps the most sickening feature of party culture.

The parties do it because "it works"; but it only works because the party system is a closed system. Americans today normally just **DO NOT HAVE THE FREEDOM** to choose well-qualified non-party candidates, except in rare and random circumstances.

We thus cannot discipline both parties at once, consistently, which is the only way to rid ourselves of this evil.

Jefferson carefully concealed his relationship to Callendar; to be publicly exposed as a source of slander against George Washington could have brought an end to his plans, if not his career as the leader of a **faction;** the co-founder of the first political party in America.

Though Jefferson carefully hid his tracks and at one point lied directly to Washington, denying in a letter any involvement with the slander, it nevertheless became generally known that he was the real leader of the anti-Federalist, hence anti-Washington, camp.

Jefferson's lie had its intended short-term effect: to "freeze" the fallout from his secret efforts to undermine Washington and to pull down the Federalist government. But the use of such a lie revealed a dishonoring element in Jefferson's character; perhaps he thought it would never be found out.

Americans recently have had to re-learn an old lesson about their elected politicians: that the habit of lying brings shame to anyone in high office; and that shame then gets reflected back onto our country.

"Our lives, our fortunes, and our Sacred Honor"

The worldview of most Americans in the 1700's was different from today in a way that made slander an issue of utmost importance. The prevalent culture in America at that time held that honor was one of the chief issues in life, was sacred. This kind of honor could be won only by doing what was understood to be right, regardless of personal cost or difficult circumstance.

The highest honor had to be earned. On the other hand, it could be lost permanently through moral failure, dishonesty or cowardice.

Public slanders in the *Aurora* and other Jefferson-leaning papers so disturbed George Washington that it made holding office unpleasant to him. He believed in the early American value of earned honor, and had based much of his career on it.

That early value system also held that honor, like love, must be freely given. It could not be demanded or coerced and still be worth anything. Washington had sworn to uphold freedom of the press. If some of his countrymen chose to dishonor or slander him, there was little choice but to endure it. But as shown in his letters and comments, it bothered him sorely.

When George Washington died three years after leaving office, the memory of these slanders lingered like open sores in Martha Washington's mind. So when Thomas Jefferson showed up at her house to publicly 'pay respects', she felt bound by custom to let him in; but was so repulsed by his visit that she later confided to a friend that it had been the "second worst day" of her life; an indication of how badly her husband's private sentiments had been afflicted by slander in the press.

Still holding to the value of honor in an earlier, pre-partyist America, and with her heart still wounded for her husband, in 1802 she named Jefferson as "one of the most detestable of mankind".

ENTER: A MORE TOXIC ATMOSPHERE

There was a clear sense in America that "things were changing". On one hand, in a newly independent republic this seemed natural, inevitable. But some of the changes were much for the worse.

THE COUNTER-CULTURE

A partisan **counter-culture** began to move in and shove aside previously healthy parts of American life.

The erosion, then near-destruction of the value American society placed on personal honor and "virtue" (excellent character) as things to be aspired to and lived up to; became casualties of this new party-ized counter-culture.

The newspapers of the period were the primary transmitters of the new counter-culture. The worst side of human nature began to assert itself, through the parties and through these papers, into the republic.

The exercise of that "rank spirit", which Washington warned against -- the spirit of accusation, invective and slander -- quickly proved to be one of the most effective ways to both advance party agendas *and* to sell papers.

But it was the emerging parties that drove the papers, not vice-versa.

Congress Investigates

At one point Jefferson secretly instigated some allies in Congress to push for an investigation of Hamilton's handling of money at the Treasury, basically accusing him of fraud. When the investigation found Hamilton completely honest, exonerating him, Jefferson would not, perhaps *could not*, accept the results, as Joseph Ellis insightfully observes.

He had become convinced that Hamilton *must* be corrupt; he would not give this idea up (again demonstrating the 'absolutist' core of his approach to nearly everything).

Jefferson simply concluded that Hamilton must be even shrewder than he'd thought.

VERSUS:
EAGLE TWO

Alexander Hamilton, Jefferson's antagonist and bete noire, was an unusual figure in history, possessing a rare order of intellect for which the word "brilliant" is not quite sufficient. Hamilton's abilities were probably closer to those of a scientist like Newton or Bacon than to his contemporaries in the military or legal professions. But his life's arc from childhood on led into the worlds of finance, law, and military organization. At these he excelled.

Though physically slight, Hamilton's insights, his command of facts, and his ability to weave those facts into a powerful argument made him formidable. To disagree with him in public, a man would run considerable risk of verbal defeat and embarrassment.

A lifetime of possessing this extraordinary intellect, no matter how well-mannered he strove to become, gave Hamilton an air of self-confidence that came off as arrogance to more than a few.

Though strictly honorable in his conduct of public business, Hamilton's vanity caused him to fall into an adulterous relationship with a woman named Reynolds, whose husband proceeded to blackmail him.

The money he was paying Reynolds became public knowledge; and Hamilton chose to confess publicly to the adulterous affair in order to make clear that he had not misused public money, only his own. In spite of the distress this caused his wife and family, such was the paramount importance of honorable conduct in a function of public trust at the time, at least in Hamilton's mind. Whether his wife or family agreed is a different question.

Fighter

Alexander Hamilton's small size and his origins, in poverty and as a reputed bastard, seem to have contributed to making him extremely sensitive to any perceived slight to his reputation. He ended up engaging in eleven different "affairs of honor" – duels – ten of them non-fatal.

Hamilton's ambition, enormous ability, energy, and penchant for sharp dress, along with his schemes for wider use of an American army (in both North and South America) with himself at the head of it, brought a comment from Abigail Adams to the effect that America could have her own Bonaparte waiting in the wings.

Lacking

For whatever reason, perhaps because of over-reliance on his intellect, Hamilton lacked some essential qualities: humility and sound judgment among them. As long as he was close to George Washington, first as a military aide then as Treasury Secretary, those deficiencies were well covered. But, significantly, Hamilton chose to keep his relationship with Washington on a somewhat formal level, what today might be described as "cordial and professional".

Hamilton's mentality led him to decline George Washington's offer of closer friendship. In explaining this decision in a letter to his father-in-law, Hamilton intimated that being viewed primarily as someone else's aide, or protégé, even someone as great as George Washington, might meet a necessity for the time; but ultimately did not fit his own concept of himself.

His long working relationship with Washington however, combined with his great abilities, made Hamilton the de facto leader of the Federalists as Washington's retirement grew near. (A majority of the Federalists – the relational network of men that led the War of Independence and supported the new Constitution, did not yet think of themselves as a "party", only as patriots.)

During his close association with Washington as a military aide, Hamilton had absorbed much of the tough-minded realism and discipline that his commander walked in. But he simply did not have George Washington's good judgment.

After Washington died, Hamilton virtually destroyed himself and his political allies through arrogance and bad judgment. He issued a toxic personal denunciation of John Adams, virtually accusing him of insanity, on the eve of the 1800 election. He was honest enough to sign his name to this denunciation; but so judgment-impaired that he apparently had no clue that it would destroy his own reputation, not Adams'; as well as destroy any political prospects in the election of 1800 for the Federalists he supposedly led.

LOW OPINIONS

Thomas Jefferson, who died bankrupt after living very well (but deeply in debt), for most of his life; held to an agrarian philosophy which envisioned the future of America as a nation of small, independent farmers; another part of his worldview centered on his personal experience, but which he thought came from Reason. He distrusted commercial interests and hated bankers.

His conviction that Hamilton was corrupt rested partly on Hamilton's plan to use federal jobs to tie the states together by giving local people a stake in the new federal government.

This appeared to Jefferson to be an exact duplicate of cronyism and corruption in the British monarchical system; there seems to have been no hint in his thinking that such a thing might be done honestly, or from good motives.

"cunning...a hypocrite"

Hamilton, on the opposing side, formed an assessment of Jefferson as "cunning" [in today's terms, "devious"]; "an intriguer", and "a hypocrite". Hamilton believed, correctly, that he was secretively forming a faction.

PARTISAN RAGS

During the time when Jefferson's alliance with James Madison was providing the nucleus for America's first political party, and Alexander Hamilton led the Federalists who were in power, another important element in the formation of partisan political culture was hard at work: the newspapers of the 1790's.

"Traitors", death warnings, and slander as treated
in 1795 Federalist political cartoon.

The first major political parties in America began to take a more defined form as popular opinion coalesced, taking sides in the battle between Hamilton and Adams' Federalists versus Jefferson and Madison's supporters (at first called "Democratic-republicans"). Party identity was increasingly interwoven with the development of these newspapers, which often functioned more like propaganda rags than providers of news.

Jefferson's propaganda through James Callendar and the Philadelphia *Aurora* proved so effective that it prompted Hamilton and others to launch their own newspapers to promote the Federalist viewpoint.

The level of venom and accusation between the camps served to harden lines of party identity among the people: favor and sympathy toward one side; anger and resentment toward the other. Jefferson, the first major party boss in American history, showed a prescient level of understanding by directing his allies, particularly James Madison, that their writings and other efforts had to aim at "the *feelings..*" of the people, not just their logic or reason.

Human nature is such that an attack against someone you agree with, or like, tends to trigger an emotional reaction in their defense. When directed against those you oppose, such attacks can easily trigger anger and resentment.

These basic human responses are constantly used and abused by parties; routinely, often cynically.

"J'accuse!" politics in France, by this time, had become a matter of life or sudden death.

"Accuse, threaten, lie and exaggerate, to win" is a capsule description for this ugly, never-ending cycle from political partisans. Little wonder the Framers used words like "poison", "rank spirit", and "disease" to describe the effects of parties in a republic.

Figure 1. "Triumph Government" c.1795 shows Jefferson trying to stop the new federal government from moving forward.

The Desperate Nature of the Struggle

It is difficult for modern people, including historians, to understand the intensity of the political battles of the 1790's. How could such eminent men of reason seem to hate and curse one another so freely? Why did such great men, all of whom are widely admired today, call each other "traitor", and worse?

Historians are human; it can take decades for such huge amounts of information as we have on the Founding era, to "sink in" and make sense.

The Founding generation had little useable concept of a "loyal opposition", a concept which later became a rationale for the party system. In their time, it was more like either someone was loyal, or *was* the opposition.

Personal loyalty was a critical element of monarchical government; it "held everything together", so to speak. Some of that habitual way of thinking carried over into the new republic.

If we can avoid the pitfall of projecting later developments backward onto an earlier time ["later developments", in this case, being the rationale for – and acceptance of – political parties], it becomes apparent that Thomas Jefferson could not have had the formation of a modern political party as his goal, even though that was the end result of his career.

So what was he doing? He was definitely "in opposition". But to understand the intensity of the struggle, on both sides, it would be more useful for a modern person to look at the struggle in terms of 'dissidents' (a faction) seeking to *overthrow the government of the United States.*

"Federalism" and "the government" were at that point nearly synonymous. The Federalists for a long time did not think of themselves as a party, but simply as patriots who had fought for Independence, and then had been elected to be the government.

But Thomas Jefferson hated Federalism; linking it in his self-made belief system with evil: with what he saw as the extension of an ancient and abusive order.

So Jefferson viewed the conflict more or less in terms of a cosmic struggle between good and evil, with himself being good, and battling great evil; which provided intensity on his side (and presumably excused his use of lying and slander as necessary means to a supposedly good end).

The truth was that the Federalists were far from "evil"; no different in that respect from other men. Many of them were in fact admirable in their character and conduct; far more so than the man (and the party) slandering them.

But this reality did not deter Jefferson from his ideology; nor did it cause him to question his own beliefs about human nature; whether the humans he applied his Reason to were black, or white.

Not enough attention has been given to the way Jefferson himself described his 1800 election win. He called it a "second revolution". A revolution is nothing less than the overthrow of an existing government or social order.

VERSUS

Triumph Government: perish all its enemies. Traitors, be warned: justice, though slow, is sure.

Figure 2. Caption for "Triumph Government" reads "Perish all its enemies. Traitors, be warned: justice, though slow, is sure."

The Federalists, on the other side, were *defending the new government of the United States,* so long fought for; so greatly labored over; with so much life and hope invested. And, in the emotional sphere, (because men are driven by emotion), the new government was precious to many of them; it was a bit like a child – their child -- still tender in many ways, thrust into a very tough world, and trying to grow up.

They correctly perceived that someone hated it and was out to do it in. We can easily see that this perception would be the main source for their intensity; though not an excuse for their tactics.

Figure 3. Detail from "Triumph Government": Dog urinates on slanderous Democratic-republican faction's newspaper.

SLANDER WARS

A slander war conducted through the newspapers of the 1790's served to harden party positions and to split society:

John Adams a Traitor?
• Jefferson's Democratic-republican side circulated the story that John Adams was secretly plotting to marry his daughter to the King of England's son so he could install the young man as Prince Regent here, and so re-establish monarchy in America.

It was an absurd slander against a great patriot; but one that a young revolutionary society could be vulnerable to.

Slave Sex?
• Federalist papers called Jefferson a "misogynist" who was secretly having sexual intercourse with one of his slaves; a seemingly outrageous libel treated by Jefferson as unworthy of reply.

Sexual exploitation occurred often enough among slaveholders to make the accusation plausible; but to throw such a charge at an honorable man like Thomas Jefferson could easily look to the public like a desperate and despicable act. Which side suffered more harm from this accusation is not easy to assess.

Jefferson successfully stonewalled the scandal. His stonewalling worked on much of the public; and even on professional historians, for two centuries; until DNA evidence lab-tested in 1998 confirmed the charge as true beyond a reasonable doubt.

Selling America Out?
• The Federalists were "Anglomen" who were intriguing (making secret agreements) with the British, said Jefferson's side, to sell out American interests.

The concept of "intrigue" popped up regularly in the 1790's. The Republic was new; in the old model, politics were conducted under monarchy. This made private agreements to oppose the crown risky, potentially even treasonous.

Intrigues (or secret agreements) might be formed, for example, to rein in a young king eager to waste resources on useless wars. Though officially deplorable, such efforts were often necessary; and could be quietly honorable.

But in the new republican context, where the people's judgment was supposed to prevail, such secret dealings could not be held to be honorable. They were highly suspect, something hidden from the people.

This charge from Jefferson's side was no less than the accusation of a deliberate Federalist betrayal of America. As a question of fact, this accusation was nonsense; but as a partisan tactic wielded in an atmosphere of turmoil and upset in a nation so new that its people were just barely learning self-government, it had its intended effect: to *undermine trust* toward the new government, and toward Federalists.

Atheist?

• Thomas Jefferson was an atheist who tried to edit and re-write the New Testament to promote his own views, charged the Federalist side. Some New England preachers predicted religious persecution if he were elected.

This charge was correct as far as the edit-and-rewrite. Jefferson made his own version of the New Testament by cutting out (physically, with a sharp knife) every reference in his copy of it to supernatural events or miracles. In private letters, he denied the divinity of Christ; and called the Gospel writers "ignorant men" who, according to Jefferson, laid out in the Gospels "..a groundwork of vulgar ignorance, of things impossible, of superstitions, fanaticisms, and fabrications."

"Of this band of dupes and imposters," Jefferson wrote, "Paul was the great Coryphaeus [chorus leader], and first corrupter of the doctrines of Jesus."[23]

---

[23] Thomas Jefferson to William Short, 13 April 1820; quoted in Waldman, *Founding Faith*, 73.

He asked his correspondents to keep his comments about Jesus and the Bible secret; so the public would not learn his actual beliefs.

Because he did believe in a God, to label Jefferson a complete atheist was false. But since he rejected the divinity of Jesus Christ, he was an atheist as far as Christian beliefs were concerned. Jefferson was not a Christian, though he represented himself as one. (In Jefferson's mind, his high regard for the moral teachings of Jesus qualified him as a "real" Christian, and allowed him to present himself that way, if it were anybody's business. Hypocrisy lay in the fact that he knew this claim would be rejected if his actual beliefs were known.)

In fact, his religious ideas were close to the teachings of Unitarianism, acknowledging a God but rejecting the divinity of Christ. Jefferson was very good at remaining a mystery; and at "playing" the religious thought patterns of his time. If his true beliefs had been known, he almost certainly would have lost the South, and therefore the Presidency.

Alexander Hamilton's assessment of Jefferson's character ("cunning [i.e., devious]…a hypocrite…") seems more and more cogent, as time passes and more of Jefferson's hidden letters come to light.

For Federalist newspapers to raise the question of whether Jefferson might initiate religious persecution, however, was wildly off-base considering his record on religious liberty. Nevertheless, it was a slander that could impact a certain segment of the population, especially in New England.

More Monarchists and Traitors?

• "Monarchists" and traitors in the Federalist party planned to establish not only a monarchy, but also a home-grown aristocracy based on money, gotten by corruption and cronyism via the new

National Bank; which would put an END to republican government and crush the common man, claimed Jefferson's side.

Based largely on fear, and on widespread ignorance of banking and of the financial realm, this oft-repeated theme included a hefty dose of self-delusion on Jefferson's part. It constituted the steadiest drumbeat in the Democratic-republican parade.

It was mostly fabrication; but it was something that Jefferson apparently believed. It was probably the second major reason that the ever-honest John Adams later said, simply,

"We were lied out of office."

The Terror in America?

• Jefferson was a "Jacobin", said the Federalist side, as evidenced by his ardent support of the French revolution even after streams of blood from the stumps of severed necks started spurting onto Parisian streets during the Reign of Terror.
Jefferson would bring the same results to America, they warned.

In the immediate sense, this was pure hyperbole. Thomas Jefferson was an ideologue; but he was an American ideologue. Winning power over his opponents was enough; he didn't need to kill them to drive home his point.

Jefferson even agreed to let the hated National Bank continue to exist, as part of his delicate dance of "arrangement" with Hamilton during the House of Representatives balloting; figuring that if he were in power, he could keep the Bank from doing too much harm. So the accusation that Jefferson might employ violence against his political opponents seems ridiculous today.

But the fear of "what Jefferson might do" was not a hollow one: he and Madison later promoted what was called the Nullification doctrine, which declared that individual states could nullify, on their own soil, any federal laws which they did not agree to. This was an early step down the road toward secession and Civil War -- the greatest bloodbath in American history.

THE TOXIC DUMP
WITH INTENT TO INJURE

Though the accusations from the Federalist side proved consistently more fact-based than the slanders from Jefferson's Democratic-republicans, their intent was no less injurious.

The verbal savagery from both sides was calculated to do injury; and that injury *was in fact taking place,* in the minds of a newly self-governing people.

It was the first large-scale toxic dump of slander and manipulation, from both parties, into the American psyche.

Parted

The virulence of these newsprint-delivered accusations divided the young country. Although the papers carrying these vitriolic articles played a major role as vehicles, there can be no historical doubt that the main thrust on each side came straight from the top. Alexander Hamilton himself wrote many damaging articles, under pseudonyms; while Jefferson and Madison closely supervised the slander campaign on their side. Madison personally wrote a number of articles, also using pseudonyms, with Jefferson directing him and suggesting topics for attack; but remaining hidden behind the scenes.

Despite Jefferson's careful use of "deniability", it was widely understood that he was the leader of the campaign. Madison was frequently called "the General" of the Democratic-republican side; but Jefferson was "the Generalissimo".

A Model of Subversion, Subverted

Jefferson and Madison were adapting—or some would say abusing--a model from before the Revolution, when "Committees of Correspondence" were set up in many locations to rapidly spread news of British injustices and American resistance efforts. These committees functioned in the time leading up to the Revolution's outbreak and the commencement of war. The purpose of the Committees was to stir up local fervor in the confrontation with England and to unify American opinion around a set of revolutionary demands and 'doctrines'.

The Committees played an enormous role in furthering the Revolution.

But what Jefferson and Madison did in the 1790's was to make use of local "Democratic Societies", which were set up to imitate the outward form of the venerable Committees; but were made vehicles of partisan ideology.

The "Democratic Societies" were designed to be pro-French, and pro-Democratic-republican.

They were being utilized to push shrill anti-government, anti-Federalist sentiment. They sowed outright enmity toward the government, using terminology that viciously equated the new American government with the old monarchical British tyranny.[24]

---

[24] Joseph Ellis, *His Excellency, George Washington*, pg. 224-225.

Deep fissures had been left in many minds by the ripping apart of colonial society; wounds which unavoidably attended the violent overthrow of British rule. Not infrequently, these wounds included breaks and strains in family relationships; or between neighbors.

To poke a sharp stick into these wounds for the sake of party advantage, to "stir hostility" to the new government in Chief Justice Marshall's words (and thus pull Federalists from office), was an integral part of the viciousness and ill will, the poisonous accusations coiled around the feet of the party system's first steps in America.

It constituted one of the earliest major toxic dumps of strife and division into the American psyche by a party. It was not done to win on a single issue; but to win on many issues by poisoning the reputations of those on the other side; and by sowing distrust.

Under the guise of replicating the Committees of Correspondence, these 'Societies' were actually pulling together a nucleus for Jefferson and Madison's Democratic-republican faction.

Polarization increased, straining not just the politics but the social fabric of the young nation. It was the advent of a very different, politicized and partisan *counterculture* -- a party culture.

America's experience of a time of new beginnings and national cohesion under George Washington was over.

JOHN MARSHALL,
The Great Chief Justice

John Marshall, the only Supreme Court Justice ever called "the great", came to thoroughly despise his cousin Thomas Jefferson. He hated what he saw being done to America.

But he was forced to hold out in a somewhat lonely vigil in the Federal court system after the election of 1800.

Marshall had had first-hand experience with the disturbing, sliming effects of partisan slander before coming to the Supreme Court.

After serving as a general in the Continental Army, he had been sent to France as a peace envoy in 1798, two years before his appointment to the Court.

In France, he and two other delegates faced months of pressure, threats, and enticements from French Foreign Minister Maurice de Talleyrand, who was attempting to extort a huge bribe before he would meet with the American delegates.

During the months of this prolonged extortion attempt, which became known as the "X, Y, Z affair", France was busy seizing dozens of American vessels on the high seas. This was when America was a baby power with virtually no navy; while France under Napoleon had become the greatest war power on earth, conquering much of Europe.

John Marshall stood firm under enormous pressure, offering friendship but refusing to pay bribes or tribute. He returned without a treaty; but he became a national hero when documents detailing the extortion attempt were published.

Before that could happen, however, he had to face smears and slander from Thomas Jefferson and party, who were mouthing the French line; and were publicly undercutting the delegation sent by President John Adams.

When the French extortion documents were published, the entire country was outraged:

"Millions for Defense, but
Not one Cent for Tribute!"

was the slogan blazed across an electrified America in response.

John Marshall was widely embraced and hailed as "The man America loves to honor". Jefferson and Madison were forced to make a hasty about-face in order to salvage their party, which they managed to do.

But John Marshall, a man of great integrity, had seen and heard enough. He detested what he witnessed being done to America through partisanship. He came to thoroughly despise, even hate, the work of Thomas Jefferson; which he judged to be deeply divisive, a faction-building approach.

After being appointed Chief Justice by John Adams, Marshall continued on the Supreme Court for thirty-five years, virtually establishing it as a co-equal branch of the government. He is the only Justice in our history to be called "the great"; called so not by official proclamation, but by widespread usage and with the agreement of his countrymen.

Fiscal Policy

Most modern economists regard Alexander Hamilton's work as Secretary of the Treasury under George Washington as having laid the essential financial foundation for a modern state; and as deserving a great deal of credit for the rapid growth of American commerce which followed.

BLESSING or CURSE?

But Jefferson and Madison opposed Hamilton's fiscal policies fiercely, and made their opposition a primary issue in pushing the formation of the country's first political party.

During the debate over the National Bank, Alexander Hamilton, who understood credit and finance, remarked that a national debt, "*if not excessive*", could actually be "a national blessing".

He was mostly referring to the establishment of good credit, which could provide a powerful instrument of safety in case of national emergency; or of opportunity, in the case of national initiatives, such as his plan to encourage American manufacturers. He also meant the benefit of tying the states more closely together, in furtherance of George Washington's goal of making the Union more secure.

But for Jefferson, this statement from Hamilton provoked revulsion, as if he'd heard some sort of slimy secular blasphemy. Madison, who orbited in Jefferson's gravitational field at this point, gave the Democratic-republican response by reviling the debt as a "national curse".

Madison was wrong at the time; but right in the long run after party politicians 200 years later made the debt hugely "excessive", turning it into a national disaster and a real curse.

The 'Head of a Faction' Wins

When the election of 1800 ended in an Electoral College tie between Thomas Jefferson and running mate Aaron Burr, (both defeating John Adams by three votes, 71-68) then became deadlocked in the House of Representatives, Hamilton made the decision to throw his influence behind his archrival Jefferson.

Jefferson's character might be flawed, Hamilton reasoned; but at least he *had* one. Burr, as far as Hamilton could see, had no character at all.

What Jefferson's ally, new Vice President Aaron Burr, did have was the foresight to carefully maintain his skill with firearms. When Hamilton later spoke too freely in public about Burr's lack of character, Burr drew him into a duel and shot him to death.

THE PARTISAN IMPACT ON AMERICA

However anyone may lean in their sympathies, toward Hamilton and the Federalists, or Jefferson's Democratic-republicans, the political and cultural results of this conflict are what truly matter: what were the consequences for America?

Among the immediate results were these: through the advent of party politics, including the use of slander and hidden manipulation; falsehood and rumor, a number of the most patriotic and able men in America were sent packing from the capitol in varying degrees of disgrace after the election of 1800.

Benjamin Franklin described John Adams as "always an honest man"; a fact almost universally acknowledged about Adams, even by those who had clashed with him (which included Franklin). After the defeat of the Federalists in the 1800 election, John Adams said simply, "We were lied out of office."

Many patriots who had born the burden of the Revolution, both intellectually and on the battlefield, were shamed and sent home, slandered as "monarchists" by the first party campaign in America. Thomas Jefferson, the first party boss, and the man who had vowed in a letter to James Madison, "I will bury Federalism into an abyss from which it will never emerge", did almost exactly that.

The man who had had his political backside kicked by Alexander Hamilton was now the one doing the kicking. Conveniently unmentioned in Jefferson's letter was the fact that "Federalism" was not merely an amorphous political philosophy; but in real human terms was the coalition of men who had led the Revolution, fought the War of Independence, and generated the Constitution of the United States.

But in party terms, within the emerging counter-culture of divisive partisan thinking, that didn't matter much. Thomas Jefferson had triumphed! and he'd triumphed by forming a faction.

Many of the men who had formed America, on the other hand, were kicked down, and out; disgraced by a new and vicious force: partisanship.

After Jefferson's gradual purge of the government, only John Marshall, the great Chief Justice, was left from the ranks of major Federalists. He went on, for 35 years, just barely protected by the Constitution from Jefferson's onslaughts, to establish American Constitutional law, for a time, as the highest standard of justice in the world; a record since ruined by mediocre political appointees to the Court.

Telling The Story

We have today a handful of excellent historians, some of the best ever to write about early America. Nevertheless, even some of these have failed us: contrary to *their* own principles, several have unwittingly fulfilled the maxim that "after a war, the winning side writes the history".

THE WINNERS

In this case, the winning side was the party system, which over time morphed into the parties-**only** system (parties only, controlling our government).

THE LOSERS

On the losing side of this history were the American people, who lost the original design of their Constitution, and lost most of their sovereignty; which was taken by the parties.

THE ENDURING IMPACT

America was now saddled with a divisive, slanderous style of politics laced with malice and accusation. The party system had been conceived, and had begun its invasive growth.

The entrenched ill will and fierce competition to which parties are prone; the division and distrust they generate; their networks of secret commitments and corruptions; and their inflated rhetoric became the ordinary backdrop of American politics.

One of the most sobering things about the supposedly protean party conflict of the 1790's is how *familiar* it all sounds to us today.

Chief Justice John Marshall watched it happening, and hated what he saw: a faction "stirring hostility to the government" as its route to power.

The Good News

The good news was that the Constitution held. Just barely. The defeated Federalists turned over power, despite feelings of bitterness and betrayal, creating an historic milestone for stable elective government.

By doing so, they established the Constitution as the law of the land just as surely as they had written it and led its ratification years before.

PART III

THE BAD NEWS

The bad news was that America was now saddled with a divisive party system which gained a permanent choke-hold over the government.

New myths came in with the *counter-culture* of partisanship. Among these myths was one which held that the two parties would somehow magically represent every viewpoint important enough to warrant representation, as a result of competing for clients.

This idea was the bankrupt equivalent of claiming that between the actions of miners and loggers, there would somehow emerge a social consensus which would benignly protect the natural environment.

Such a myth contradicted the political reality captured succinctly by John Adams after the election of 1800:

> "Jefferson had a party," Adams said, "Hamilton had a party, but the commonwealth had none."[25]

Just as some men were heedlessly ripping and raping the natural realm, leaving blighted landscapes behind; other men were ripping and toxic-dumping the American psyche with their savage partisan wars; with lies and slanders and poisonous character assassination; leaving behind a devastated and blighted political landscape.

The triumph of partisanship means that Americans, from early on, have experienced a distorted version of what representative government should be.

---

[25] Ellis, *Founding Brothers*, 204.

The party system, among other things, has forced voters into a crude and dysfunctional "government by lurches" back-and-forth party-choice pattern in which the people's will cannot prevail smoothly, but must always be thwarted in matters important to them.

The party system has also injected a non-Constitutional layer of lobbyists and brokers between the people and their government. Corruption, cronyism, waste and crushing debt follow on the list of results for parties-only government, after more than two hundred years of experience.

Such things are not simply the results of representative government, as failed historians and editorial writers would have us believe; they are results of the party system.

The party system, as we've experienced it, does not work. It started out "broken", based on enmity, lying and slander; and on "flipping" the elected representatives of the people over into becoming representative agents of the parties. The party system started out rotten, but in recent times has gotten worse: it is now an oppressive, vexing burden on America.

The party system is like a hundred-pound tumor; mimicking healthy tissue and absorbing nutrients; but producing little (aside from dead weight) that would not have been done much better under the Framers' original Design. It has only lasted this long because of the immense strength of its "host": the American people; American culture; and our Constitutional form of government.

And it has only lasted because, as a system, it has had no real competition. *The party system is corrupt and tottering,* ready to burst like an economic bubble once it is presented with a sturdy source of free competition.

If America becomes weakened, for whatever reason, she will suddenly realize how much this tumor called the party system has drained from her; and the immense loss of energy and treasure she has suffered. *TRILLIONS* in debt, is the most easily measured effect. But there are other, unseen effects which are worse.

TAINTED

The dumping of toxic (party) waste into the American psyche is the most damaging and lasting of these effects. Many Americans have had their *thinking* tainted when it comes to politics. Where our thinking should ideally be clear, a dark tint of anger, anxiety, and hatred hover at the edge of many minds, as is evident in our public discourse.

Otherwise intelligent people speak today (and appear to think) in degrading terms of enmity and anger; of "fighting for" this or "fighting against" that; without questioning what their own attitude has become, or where it came from.

"No man is an island," says the proverb; and it is true that all humans are to one degree or another steeped in a culture, for good or ill.

Our political culture has been deeply tainted; *diseased* by a divisive, accusative habit of thought; evidence of the pervasive effect on us of unrelenting partisanship. This kind of thinking, in any century or culture, brings the disintegration of societies; it destroys social trust.

Just as surely as parties have destroyed republics in the past, our party system now is dragging America toward failure. It has simply taken our parties longer to do it because the Framers' design slowed them down.

But they have found the way to do it: by consolidation of power into fewer and fewer hands, with small knots of party leaders acting more and more like oligarchs; by stirring constant enmity and resentment among the people; by the obscene dominance of money over party politicians; by lying; by cynical manipulation of the public; by bitter partisanship ending in gridlock; and by heedlessly and selfishly creating enormous tar-pits of unbearable public debt into which future generations will be born already stuck, ruining their fair share of the experience of freedom.

"PARTIES-ONLY"

The phrase "parties-only" is intended to spotlight a twisted distortion which has become so familiar to us that we no longer perceive it, or think much about it: Our government is controlled by parties. Only.

Not "parties plus journalists"; not "parties plus scholars and experts"; and certainly not "parties plus citizens". No. Parties, only, control our governments.

This parties-only system must be presented with a permanent source of free competition, if we are ever to break its two-headed monopolistic hold.

But third, fourth, or fifth parties cannot accomplish this: they would only *multiply* the evils of the present party system: <u>more</u> parties, <u>more</u> insider deals, <u>more</u> gridlock, etc.

Only when the people have their Right restored to nominate their own candidates for public office, will there exist a free-choice election system which will provide **real** competition to the parties, in the form of *non-party* candidates in every election. Thereby enabling the voters *at last!* to discipline both parties at once by voting them both out at once, whenever they choose.

When the voters can discipline both parties at once, then they will finally be able to rid themselves of liars and spinners (instead of being forced to merely reward an alternate set of liars and spinners--the other party. That has been the voters' only option under the parties-only system).

When the voters can discipline both parties at once, then they will finally be able to crush hubris and aim the flamethrowers of their votes into the spider holes of party money brokers; and to *kick out* the promoters of the negative, the vile, and the venomous, who currently ruin our public discourse.

In the context of Liberty, parties cannot be banished; as the Framers knew. They can be disciplined by the voters; but only if the voters have a **non**-party alternative to vote *for*.

CHAPTER EIGHT

The Power of Organization

It took the emerging, organized parties less than two decades to trample over and cast aside most of the checks and restraints which the Framers' original design appointed for them. With our vantage point of experience, we are now able to understand the reasons why the parties could do it so easily. These reasons are straightforward, not mysterious or complex.

World history has shown over and over the sheer power of *organization* in human affairs.

In politics, and particularly in the politics of a representative government, an un-organized (and sometimes unaware) population is no match for determined groups which mobilize; and when unchecked by any counterbalancing force, can persistently coordinate their efforts and statements to win elections.

Party Organization in America

In looking back at the development of parties during the early, post-Revolution stage of the Republic, we would conclude that one of the primary fathers of party strategy in America was Aaron Burr, an amoral, womanizing power-seeker. Burr, later charged with treason, was a formative influence in the Tammany Hall political machine; who in the election of 1800 innovated and organized some of the very first voter turnout drives and rallies in New York state on behalf of himself and his ally Thomas Jefferson; turnout drives which very likely won that state (and ultimately the presidency) for Jefferson.

But regardless who gets credit for it, it is this "boots on the ground" strategy to raise money and *organize* party manpower to win elections which is the key to this period of history, and to the astonishing rise of political parties. They rose, as it were, from the bottom of a pit – the open, public contempt of the Framers – inexorably upward, first to electoral success and then to their ultimate prize: complete control of American government.

"Organize, Organize!"

Vladimir Lenin's motto – and method -- for the Communist Party to seize control of all Russia was, "Organize! Organize, Organize!" The coordinated effort of a unified group toward a single goal is an incredibly powerful force, especially when the "mass" of the people is *un-organized* or unaware.

It is no wonder then that the first political parties in America were able to rapidly get control of the government. No evil intent was necessary, as with the Communists; no ideology of murder and confiscation.

But there was a direct parallel, in terms of human behavior.

In retrospect, it was inevitable: the parties needed only to <u>organize</u> and be persistent, while proclaiming policies (at least in public) that voters could accept.

The people had no more chance of stopping the parties than a peaceful population equipped only with rakes and hoes would have in stopping a professional army from marching into their land. The point of this simile is not the "invasion". It is the *power of organization,* directed against an unorganized and unprepared people.

We must learn from history in the same way the Framers did. The lesson of history is this: an organized group, even though small in number, but exerting a united effort toward a single goal, is more than a match for a much larger number of people who are unorganized; and who may be unaware of the nature of the contest underway, often thinking it to be only an election for one office.

Like the Framers did, we must apply the lessons of history to our republic and to our Constitution.

The Lesson of History

One of the greatest lessons of history to re-emerge in these last two centuries is the enormous, predominating power of organization in human affairs.

Good organization determines the effectiveness of transport systems, armies, corporations, athletic teams – and almost every other joint effort that men undertake.

The Party Conquest of America's Government: From Outside the Framework

Many Americans today are surprised to learn that the Constitution does not give any formal role in government to political parties. None. The Constitution does not give parties, as such, any standing.

The parties have taken their role from outside the Constitutional framework, as private clubs with their own agendas: by *organizing* (like entrepreneurial businesses or athletic clubs might) to compete in elections – a development which may seem obvious in hindsight to us who have suffered so long with "Government *of* the parties, *by* the parties, and *for* the parties' special interests".

But the Framers had no way to anticipate this development. No one on earth in their time had seen it happen. Nor had anyone seen how elections would work out in a large republic.

A majority of Americans today have no idea that the Framers of the Constitution loathed and distrusted political parties. Most have no idea that the Framers put enormous thought and effort into writing the Constitution so as to constrain and limit the effects of "party" in American government.

Despite the Framers' careful work, it took the newly organized parties less than two decades to overcome most of their Constitutional restraints, trash several major provisions of the original Design, and take control of American government.

Consequently, Americans in our time simply do not know what kind of republic the Framers tried to design; because we have never seen it operate in its intended form.

Political Parties Are
Not In the Constitution

The simple truth that the Constitution gives no role in government to political parties must be brought home to the American people, so that they may free their minds from a lifetime of mental conditioning; and from an abyss of ignorance fostered by failed historians.

This, toward the goal that they may become fully persuaded that it is both necessary and possible to restore the original design of the American Constitution.

The Unresolved Problem

When we finally arrive at this understanding about *how* and *why* parties were able to trample over the Framers' design [by operating from outside of that design; and through the sheer power of organization, focused on winning elections]; and in the course of seeking to *restore* the Framers' original design; we will find ourselves facing the same dilemma the Framers faced:

> How do you limit the effects of political parties
> in a free republic without destroying, or in any way
> diminishing, the rights and liberties of party members?

Two hundred years of electoral experience have slowly yielded answers to this dilemma from a perspective the Framers did not – and could not -- have.

CHAPTER NINE

The Intent of Restoration

In seeking to restore the Constitution's original design, our intention is not merely to restore details; even a detail as important as the selection method for U.S. senators.

Nor is the intention to destroy political parties: that was not the Framer's approach.

Our intention must be clearly defined:

Since parties in some form will always exist in a free republic, there must be created a Constitutional mechanism which will perpetually
GIVE THE PEOPLE THE UPPER HAND OVER THEM,
as the Framers intended and tried to do in their design.

Parties-Only In Control: The Ruin of America

The parties-only system is ruinous.

The power of parties must be checked. In the context of liberty, parties must be *balanced out* by an alternative NON-party source of electoral power.

Checks and balances are the genius of our Constitutional design.

The unjust domination by organized parties over our elections must be **checked** on a permanent basis, in order for our Republic to survive.

Party domination is *unjust,* destructive *and anti-freedom* because the effect of it is to rob Americans of their liberty to nominate and their right to elect **non**-party candidates whenever they would choose to do so.

Unfair party domination of elections is *immoral* because its effect is to steal the choicest portion of the people's sovereignty and siphon it to party leaders.

The effects of party domination over our elections must be *controlled,* in the words of *Federalist #10,* by creating a permanent source of free, *non*-party competition to act as a check and balance to all parties. That **check** being the Right to Nominate Amendment, written into the Constitution; and the *balance* to be determined in every election by the votes of the American people.

The parties-only system must be changed to a "people-and-parties" system, [meaning that **non**-party candidates may be freely brought forward by the people and nominated, completely *apart and separate* from party influences; then placed on the final ballot alongside party candidates].

Such a Constitutional system will not banish or destroy parties; but will give the people the upper hand over them: *which was the original design, the intention,* of the Framers. This must happen before America is lost.

This change will require the Constitutional amendment which restores a lost right—the Right to Nominate--to Americans, thereby putting this right beyond the manipulations of party politics.

When Americans can nominate their own candidates for public office, when their liberty is expanded so they can vote for people they'd really *choose* to vote for, instead of being handed their own shackles in the form of party-designated lists of party candidates, then we will have **a** Constitutional check to all parties, a new balance in our elections that will *break* the corrupt control, the stranglehold, that parties presently have over our government.

When Americans are finally set free to seek out and vote for excellent NON-party candidates, then the monstrously inflated party "bubble", with all its abuses, will be burst.

Parties will not disappear; but their arrogance and overweening power will be drastically reduced. They will have to compete for office, not just with each other, but with the high, real standards of American voters; voters who are *sick of party politics* and who will now have perpetual access to the most accomplished and respected private citizens in America to cast their votes for.

That ongoing access to excellent non-party candidates will continue, after adoption of the Amendment, to form a baseline for our elections.

This will continue to happen because a permanent pathway will have been designated by this Amendment for respected and highly capable citizens to be *invited,* in each election, to become candidates for public office through the people's Right to Nominate.

THE LOST RIGHT

The Amendment to restore this lost right, the Right to Nominate, must adhere exactly to the principles of liberty and inalienable rights which guided the Framers. This means, among other things, that the rights and liberties of party members must not be infringed.

Restoring this lost Right to all Americans will not only preserve our liberties; it will expand them.

From the Constitution's standpoint, if one or both of the current major parties were to wither away and disappear, it would be no great loss. Such a development could, in fact, be of considerable short-term benefit by giving an amended *checked-and-balanced* election system a better chance to take root.

But there is little or no chance of such a development happening quickly enough to offer an unfettered start to an amended system. This amended system will have to make its way through open, possibly bruising, competition with the parties, in the context of liberty; completely dependent on the support and approval of American voters.

But if one or both of the current major parties *were* to disappear, providing a short-term benefit, not much would be gained in the long run. New parties would simply spring up to replace the ones discarded. This cycle has been repeated several times in American history.

CHAPTER TEN

Parties

Parties are inevitable. They spring from human nature. At their most basic level, parties are simply products of the human ability to co-operate, to organize joint effort toward a common goal. This capability is obviously one of the most powerful innate attributes of the human race.

Hunting parties are vastly more effective than individual hunters, especially when large game is the target. The building of houses or large community structures requires this powerful human capability to co-ordinate efforts, as does almost every other major area of human endeavor.

So why did the Framers have such "a problem" with parties, as found in republics?

The Framers were realists. James Madison's remark, "If men were angels, no government would be necessary" accurately summarizes one of their core assumptions. *[Federalist #51 (4)]*

Men are not angels. The human record contains an appalling mixture of the noble and the horrific. For any plan of government to be successful, the Framers reasoned, it must deal with men as they are; not as someone might hope or theorize they could be. Historical results were their yardstick, their measuring device for determining the usefulness of design proposals for government.

In theory, parties are neither good nor evil in themselves; they, like individuals, must be evaluated by their *results*. But the results of political parties, as the Framers found over and over in examining the history of republics, were horrible; were catastrophic. The effects of factions and parties operating in the Framers' own time were also terribly damaging.

So in theory, parties *could* be beneficial. But their actual record throughout history has been extremely destructive to republics. They have repeatedly descended into the lowest and most vile flaws of human nature – slander, divisiveness, greed and hatred -- and produced more and more strife in the pursuit of partisan advantage.

George Washington's warning against parties described one key reason why this is so: parties are the most effective means by which a small number of unelected and unaccountable men can, through the network of obligation and advantage found in a party, gain a great measure of control over an elected government and use that control from behind the scenes for their own ends.

Parties exist primarily to gain something for their members and supporters. For some, this gain may be psychological – the triumph of a point of view. But for others, the possible gains in terms of money, contracts, power and fame are so enormous that they become willing to use any tactic or practice, no matter how vile or unprincipled, to achieve their goals.

With such stakes in view, it is no wonder that parties fight "like hell"; and throughout history, have dragged whole city-states and nations into ruin.

DIVIDE TO WIN

Experience has taught us one essential fact about political parties: they *divide* society by representing conflicting interests in a dysfunctional, unhealthy way as seen from the standpoint of community.

In our own experience, parties have represented conflicting interests in such a way as to *perpetuate* the conflicts rather than heal them.

They then derive money and manpower from relentlessly harping on the conflicts they help perpetuate. So our society frequently gets "churned" by the parties not to solve problems, but to benefit those doing the churning.

Rhetoric

Party rhetoric is notoriously divisive. Party politicians constantly speak of "fighting" for this and "fighting" for that. We have gotten so used to the rhetoric of these "fighting fools" that we are almost deaf to it: a mark of the futility that has become built in to party-system politics.

Who are they fighting? Their rhetoric suggests huge, malevolent forces; but human reality tells us that these 'forces' inevitably boil down to other Americans who disagree with them.

This form of rhetoric constantly takes advantage of a weakness in human nature. All humans are "wired" to react to danger, to threats. By constantly stirring and provoking this natural reaction to threat (often by rhetorically manufacturing it); and by interpreting problems in terms of division and fighting, the parties take advantage of this human weakness to motivate people to support their causes.

Of course, one byproduct of this execrable pattern (i.e., taking advantage of a human weakness) is to install party politicians and leaders in places of great influence and power. From where they can then battle the huge malevolent threat of other Americans disagreeing with them.

The problem for voters, for the people, is to discern between real threats and rhetorical, manufactured ones.

It Just Keeps Getting Worse

But since both parties benefit from this pattern of "conflict maintenance" and the rhetoric of "fighting", they have little reason to change it. The two parties will likely continue the pattern (and make it steadily worse) until the people gain the ability to discipline them both by voting them both out at the same time.

Having the ability to discipline only one party at a time (by voting **it** out and another party in) actually *rewards* the other party for doing the same divisive, manipulative things as the first. So the cycle has become perpetual.

Lurches

This cycle also produces "government by lurches", a very inefficient, crude form of representative government which does not truly represent the steady, ongoing will of the people. At best, it represents only a part of that will at a time.

The overall result is that an astounding proportion of the actual will of the people must be thwarted at any given time, partly because some of that will tends to reside in each party. Although this is frustrating to most of the people, it turns out to benefit both parties. Protracted, unresolved conflicts, and divisions which hang on and on, act as a fuel source for them.

Over time, this crude result creates such frustration in the people that it could precipitate a catastrophic and unwarranted turning away from representative government itself, on the grounds that "it doesn't work".

It is not representative government which "doesn't work": it is the *party system,* in which parties <u>only</u> control the government.

Parties are able to maintain control because of the simple fact that party candidates, or an occasional self-nominated soul, are the only ones that the people are *able* to vote for: a tremendous **curtailment** and **restriction of freedom**. It is this party-organized, party-benefitting electoral system which forces voters into a crude "government by lurches" pattern.

Electoral "lurching" is the only available means the voters have to discipline either party.

MADISON'S THEORY OF PARTIES IN AMERICA

James Madison theorized in *Federalist #10* that a republic as large as America would be safer than the small historical republics of Greece and Italy because (he thought) no one would be able to cobble together such an enormous number of different interest groups as America had, into a working political entity. He should have been right. In theory, he was right.

But in practice, the emerging parties walked all over his theory, trampling it into political pig mire.

The major reason for this was the parties-**only** system itself. Once the parties took hold, the people had no other choice: it was either one party or another, with no **non**-party alternative; no organized way to curb them both.

On a few occasions in American history, a new party emerged, seeming to offer some hope for change. But apart from offering changes on particular issues, these parties then slipped right into the same pattern of what can only be called an historic regime, the "parties-only" (in control of government) regime. They just became newer pieces of the same old pattern.

If the people had had a mechanism to nominate non-party candidates from the beginning, the parties would not have been able to compel compliance from so many disparate interests (as Madison hoped would be the case).

The party argument to interest groups has been, "If you want to get your priorities met, then you have to *go along* with us; and go along with many other groups 'getting theirs' also; even if you disagree with (or hate) their agendas."

The "go along to get along" ethic of party politics is a prime reason our government has become bloated, sprawling, over-intrusive and resistant to change.

But if the people had had the power from the beginning to nominate non-party candidates and the means to do so, then the coercive arguments of the parties would never have gotten off the ground. James Madison's theory would have been vindicated; and the American people would not have lost most of their sovereignty.

CLAMOR

The second reason Madison's theory was overturned in practice was the power of clamor: cries of accusation and alarm without true basis. Since the beginning of American independence, such party cries have had a visceral, divisive effect.

Parties thrive on conflict, and on unhealed wounds. They benefit organizationally if those wounds are poked and reopened over and over.

They could have thrived by seeking to heal such wounds, but their core leaderships have never thought this way. It seems written in party DNA: *"to destroy your opponents or utterly subdue them is the key to problem-solving."*

It is only a short step for ideologues and partisans at the core of parties to assume that those who oppose their agendas are not just fellow citizens with a different viewpoint, but are more than likely the enemy who *causes* the problems.

They have not changed in this essential element of their mentality since the 1790's, whether one calls this trait "spiritual DNA"; or "a self-deluding viewpoint, steeped in conflict, passed down by party traditions."

The Foul Breath, Updated

One of the most corrupt ideas ever produced by party mentality has emerged recently: the idea that "personal character and morality don't really matter in officeholders; only their stands on issues".

Following this logic, we could elect thieves, liars, racketeers, drug users, adulterers, swindlers, pedophiles and lunatics to public office, and the government would work just fine as long as they all voted and acted according to their party's line.

But where would the "party line" come from?

Who would "issue" it?

This idea is worse than moronic; it is lethal. It would bring death to any republic.

It would concentrate power into a tiny number of oligarchs: the few who determine what the "party line" is; and would disenfranchise all others, including officeholders.

Whoever would espouse such a thing has shown contempt for the entire thought process of the Framers and would earn the scorn of his or her country. This idea should be treated for what it is: the foul breath of amorality; a preliminary whiff of the stench and decay of despotism.

Revulsion

Recognizing the reality of such corrupt thinking; and the endlessly recycled tactics of division and manipulation which issue from parties—which are no accident, but are "encoded" in their DNA-- triggers the same revulsion, along with a great temptation to banish or destroy them, that the Framers experienced.

But the Framers had the right approach. Parties spring from human nature; and conflicts will exist as long as human nature remains as it is. And people must be free to associate with whom they choose, and to join their efforts together toward mutual, lawful goals.

As much as they loathed parties, the Framers did not set out to banish or destroy them. Put simply, they valued liberty more than they hated parties.

Our Constitutional goal, therefore, must be to limit the harm parties can do, (which was the Framers' approach) and to maximize their *potential* benefits.

The goal must be to channel their tremendous energy toward positive service (which would be honest representation); and away from the worst potentials of human nature: divisiveness, ill-will, insider corruption, manipulation of voters, enmity, slander, election fraud and other vile practices.

PART IV

CHAPTER ELEVEN

The Crux

The party system, as we've experienced it, does not work. Parties-**only** as a form of government has slowly been grinding America down toward political paralysis; and toward becoming the economic equivalent of an enormous beached whale, with its strength drained, gasping for breath under a crushing weight of debt.

The party system is emphatically *not* what the Framers designed or intended for America. In fact, this concept was repulsive, abhorrent to them. They tried their best to prevent it from happening.

The effects of the parties-only system have brought America horribly close to failure.

But the answer to this terrible and dangerous situation lies in the Framers' approach: more rights and liberties for Americans, not less.

ONLY WHEN:

Only when voters have, in every election, choices on their ballot other than (meaning "in addition to") party candidates will they be able to discipline *all* parties into positive service and away from vile practices.

A Third Party Is No Answer

Third parties cannot provide an answer to this terrible situation. Third, fourth, or fifth parties only provide **more** parties; they *multiply* the discord and insider corruption of a "parties-only" system. Americans historically have been wise to steer away from the political snake-ball of multi-partyism.

The parties-only system *is* the problem; whether there are two, five, or twenty of them. It is the "only" in "parties-only" that makes it not work.

NO OTHER WAY

Since parties spring from human nature, it must be concluded that they will spring up and exist wherever there is free, elective government.

This being true (and it has proven to be so in every free republic established during the past two hundred years) then the only way to provide a counter-balance to party dominance of *any* free government is to provide a Constitutional mechanism for the people to nominate *other, non-party candidates* for public office. To nominate private citizens who are not agents or representatives of any party.

Then, in the general elections, let all the voters choose between the party candidates (whether there are two parties or ten); and these non-party, citizen-nominated candidates.

The Timeless (AND ONLY) Answer

There is no other way for voters in a free election venue to force change upon both (or, or in multiparty nations, all) parties.

Given a choice in every election between party vs. **non**-party candidates, the people will eventually find their own preferred balance; they will end up choosing what they think is the right proportion of each.

But when sufficient numbers of non-party candidates have been freely nominated and elected, then the balance of power will be put back into the hands of the people, and the "parties-*only*" regime of government that has dominated and corrupted America for over two centuries will come to an end.

After that, secret commitments made behind closed doors by oligarchs in the parties will cease to be the final decisions over American government that they have been up to now. Even if parties persist in making these secret commitments (which they will: it's encoded in their DNA), the people will now have the leverage, through *their own* elected representatives to fully review (to approve or disapprove) such commitments before they can become law.

Parties will not come to an end. But parties-<u>only</u> in control as a form of government, as a regime, must and will end.

Then we will be able to say, "Government of the people, by the people, and for the people *has not perished* from the earth!" ...but not before then.

This approach treasures and preserves Liberty, the overarching value that motivated the Founders, as the great context for our elections.

It will finally put the ultimate decision--the choice *to nominate* who will represent them--in the hands of the voters as the Framers intended, not in the hands of those who make up party lists or nominate themselves.

EXPANDING LIBERTY

In truth, this approach toward a restored, Constitutionally sound electoral system *expands* liberty by giving voters the freedom to vote for someone other than those few persons on the lists of party politicians plus self-nominated souls that we have been forced to choose from for so long in primary as well as general elections.

Party-based elections severely restrict the freedom of Americans to vote for whom they would truly *want* to vote for, and would *choose* to vote for, if they had the chance.

If each voter could survey his or her entire community and pick out whom they thought to be the most honest and trustworthy persons; the most capable; and those most deserving of respect, to become candidates for public office, then you would come close to the Framers' ideal system for a republic. In fact, you would have the kind of republic the Framers tried to design!

Instead, time and again, voters are forced to choose between two or more unsatisfactory *party* candidates imposed upon them by the party system. Being forced to choose "the lesser of two evils" is not liberty, as the Founding Generation fought to establish it. It is, instead, an intolerable *restriction* of liberty!

Being handed a small list of party candidates and self-nominated souls; and being told that these are the ones you are allowed to choose from (or waste your vote on a useless write-in), *is not liberty.* It is a party-organized, party-benefitting, ugly and intolerable *restriction* of American liberty!

"Hold your nose, and pull the lever" is the advice from cynics; but the cynics are not far from the mark, in the minds of most Americans.

Many people of integrity (when looked at as potential candidates for public office, in a future, amended, *checked-and-balanced* election system) do *not* fit in with party culture, nor are they willing to subject themselves to party agendas and to the slanderous, degrading campaigns which now dominate our political marketplace under the parties-only system.

THE ONE WEAK POINT

The Framers' failure to foresee the need for checks and balances in the election system was the one weak point in their otherwise marvelous design.

History has consistently shown that small, determined and organized groups can easily overwhelm a larger population of *un-organized* people, whether it be in military campaigns, elections, or the marketplace. And that's what happened in America.

It has taken us two hundred years to finally grasp this simple, universal principle and apply it to an understanding of our own history. We find ourselves facing not some mysterious "historical force", nor some conspiratorial mindset but a simple, straightforward reality of human behavior which operates so consistently that it approaches the status of a law of nature: A small *organized* group, in any venue, will almost always prevail over an un-organized, larger population.

By not providing a genuine **check** or *balance* to organized party domination of elections, the Framers unknowingly left America and her blessedly unorganized people, as well as the unorganized peoples of every republic formed since, vulnerable to the very thing they detested: party domination; and the warping effect on culture of *"party spirit"*.

This pattern has been repeated in virtually every free republic established since the American Revolution. This pattern is unjust on its face: because it is predicated on restricting voters' ability to vote for candidates they'd *want* to vote for and would *choose* to vote for; by simply never giving them the chance.

CHOICE?

The idea that being forced to choose between slates of *party-nominated* candidates constitutes real freedom of choice is pathetic and delusional. How many honest and capable independent persons are we **not free** to vote for because they *never appear on a party-organized ballot?*

Tens of thousands, at least.

SHOULD WE GET MORE DRASTIC?

A more drastic solution to this unjust, immoral *organized* party domination of elections could be adopted, such as constitutionally limiting the number of seats parties may hold in our legislatures.

This approach would appear to achieve the valid objective of giving the people the upper hand over the parties. It should not be permanently ruled out in case a future generation should feel forced to adopt such a measure.

But from the Framers' standpoint, attaining even a valid objective by such means could only come at the expense of liberty. Such a cost was unacceptable to them. That was not their approach.

The Framers did *all* their work in the context of liberty as the prime solution.

To restore and complete their magnificent design, then, we must accomplish our goal by holding liberty as the primary context exactly as the Framers did.

In fact, only by *expanding* liberty so that Americans are able to vote *for whom they'd truly and spontaneously choose,* to *become* candidates for public office (i.e., to be nominated); as opposed to routinely encountering lists of party politicians as the only eligible candidates, can we restore the Framers' original design and recover the lost sovereignty of the people.

CHAPTER TWELVE

The Cornerstone Uncovered

Establishing a constitutional mechanism for Americans to nominate their own non-party candidates is not just 'an idea'. It rests on the discovery of a timeless principle; a principle *transcendent* in power and importance for the future of Western democracies.

This principle is far greater, far more important, than any set of temporary reforms could be; but until now it has been buried, unseen, in the nomination process.

There is a *Right* of the people buried in our nomination rituals without which free, representative government can not develop properly; or reach full maturity.

The deeper one looks into this model [a constitutional mechanism for the people to nominate their own non-party candidates], the more this previously hidden and presently unredeemed right begins to emerge into the light.

THE RIGHT

It is the Right to Nominate. This Right *belongs* to the people.

But the Right has been withheld from the people, mindlessly usurped; eagerly appropriated by parties (and individuals) for their own use.

This usurping didn't happen because of some massive conspiracy or deliberately evil mindset.

It happened because the ability, or right, to nominate was simply there for the taking. Practical men, organizing to win elections, were more than happy to grab hold of it and use it. The Right to Nominate was completely unprotected.

As a revolutionizing force, the Right to nominate was neglected. And through ignorance, it was *undirected* (not put to universal use, nor into a highly productive form) because it was not recognized for what it is: *a right of the people.*

As long as the parties got what they wanted out of it [control of the government], they were happy to leave things as they were; and to leave the people in ignorance, with the choicest part of their sovereignty already gone: quietly pocketed by the parties.

THE MISSING CORNERSTONE

This right, the Right to Nominate, is the missing cornerstone of representative government, the essential element without which the people **can't** exercise sovereignty.

(It is also the unrecognized object of Amendment IX in the American Constitution.)

THE ESSENTIAL MISSING RIGHT:
SECOND DEDICATION

In the course of restoring the original design of the Constitution, this book is also

Dedicated

*To recovering the missing piece, an Article
omitted, from the Bill of Rights:*

The Right to Nominate

That is, dedicated to recovering a hidden but fundamental right of the people which will prove to be the key component for restoring the Constitution's original design. Indeed, this unredeemed Right is *the* indispensible component for completing the foundation of representative government itself.

THE UNKNOWN RIGHT

No one on earth in the Framers' time had had experience with repeated elections in a large, free republic. So the information necessary to discern this hidden right was simply not available.

But after two hundred years of electoral experience, this information is now ours. Our experience has gradually revealed the existence of this right. Experience has slowly brought it into the light.

Like The Secret of Flight

Like the secret of flight, which eluded men for thousands of years although its use was demonstrated almost daily in front of their eyes, this principle – this Right – has been *"hidden in plain sight"* for centuries:

***It is the Right of the people to nominate
candidates for public office.***

145

To nominate their own candidates, not merely be forced to choose from somebody else's list. In our case, that has been a list of party members and self-nominated souls.

The people must be able to *initiate* nominations in order to exercise this Right; not merely be presented with a list of party reps to "choose" from.

Such a party list *restricts* the choices of the people, and robs them of their right to engage in the first, and most determinative, stage of election. It robs them of their right to make *their own* lists to choose candidates from. Party-generated lists usurp this right, and the end result is to steal from the people what is theirs: their sovereignty.

CHAPTER THIRTEEN

The Nominating Power

In any elective system, whoever controls the nomination of candidates for public office ultimately controls the resulting government. If this ultimate lever of power is not in the hands of the people (their Right); then it must be in the hands of an autocrat; or in the hands of one party; or in the hands of small (and by definition, elite) groups.

Examples of such elite groups would include hereditary aristocracies; committees of religious mullahs; or, as has often been the case in our own experience, the inner rings and activist cores of political parties.

The motives and methods of such "inner ring" groups may vary tremendously; ranging from genuine benevolence and public service, to outright tyranny: to rank despotism.

But the underlying principle does not vary. It remains the same regardless of differences in culture or differences in historic time periods. *Wherever* or *whenever* there is an elective system of government, this principle operates as simply as a law of nature:

Whoever controls nominations for public office will control the resulting government.

The right to this hidden lever of power – the power to nominate – belongs to the people.

Revealed by History

Two centuries of electoral experience here and abroad has gradually shown that the "right to vote" actually consists of two parts: the right to nominate, and the right to elect. The right to elect (the more visible of the two) is in reality subject to the other less examined part: the Right to Nominate.

Nearly every dictatorship and sham "republic" in the last century has guaranteed its citizens the right to vote. The Cubans, Chinese and Iranians today; the citizens of the former Soviet Union and East Bloc, all have had a <u>guaranteed</u> right to vote; that is, to elect. They can vote "for anyone they choose", provided, of course, that the person has been *nominated* (by the real power) and appears on the ballot. The only question, obviously, is: Who controls the nominations?

When separated from the Right to Nominate, the right to 'vote' – to elect – becomes at the very least, impaired; but at worst, it becomes cruel manipulation; a deceptive tool of tyranny over the people.

These two rights are inseparable; and both belong to the people.

"Retained by the People"

This missing unredeemed right, the Right to Nominate, can in hindsight be understood to have formed an underlying motive for Amendment IX to our Constitution -- unconsciously, because the Right was unrecognized and therefore not able to be described at that time. No one on earth then had sufficient electoral experience to discern or describe it.

Nevertheless, sensing that something was missing, that some unknown things were not covered by their new Document, and determined that future generations must not lose rights simply because of their inexperience, the Founding generation took a determined stand with Amendment IX of the Bill of Rights:

> IX. *The enumeration in the Constitution, of certain rights, shall not be construed to deny or disparage others retained by the people.*

What we hear in Article IX is not the voice of an academic or of legal scholars.

What we hear is the tough, determined voice of a war generation who risked their lives and fortunes to defend their rights and who were determined not to allow them to be taken away again, ever.

When read with that Founding war generation in mind, Amendment IX rumbles forward to us through time like the distant mighty thunder of the American Revolution.

Who Owns This Right?

That the Right to Nominate exists has been gradually revealed over time. That this Right belongs to the people and not to lordly individuals nor to self-ordained private clubs[26] (i.e. parties) lusting for power, is undeniable.

That this Right has been unprotected and its exercise *by the people* un-provided for; which in turn has led to its being usurped, used and abused for both good and ill by a variety of groups since the early days of our Republic, is a matter of record.

---

[26] "Clubs", an accurate word, is cribbed from Mickey Edwards, *The Parties versus The People*.

Thomas Peterson

The Missing Piece of the Framers' Design

The lesson made unmistakable by our history is that by not providing a constitutional mechanism for the people to reach into their own communities to nominate candidates for public office, independent from all parties, the Framers' marvelous and enduring structure of government became like a ripe, low-hanging fruit available for picking by whatever groups *organized* themselves most effectively to commandeer and use the Right to Nominate for themselves. And then charge unchecked onto the field of electoral battle, the "winner to take all".

The spoils to be taken were enormous: control of the two electoral branches of government (including control of government revenues); and possible control of the third.

For the parties to grab and use the Right to Nominate was in itself not a crime: political parties have as much right to nominate candidates as any other private club or individual does, no more and no less. Their right to nominate their own candidates to promote their own agendas should not be infringed.

The True Exercise of Liberty

The issue is: Whether any others (meaning not "other parties"; but "others" as in "the overwhelming, vast majority of the people") have the *opportunity* or the *means* to exercise this right as well. To nominate their own candidates and thus provide a Constitutional check by offering a choice -- an *alternative to party candidates* – in every general election.

Let the people have the means to nominate whatever candidates they will; and then let the parties nominate whatever candidates *they* will. Let all these nominated candidates be placed on the ballot for a general election.

Then, let the whole body of citizens decide who to elect.

That will be a true exercise in liberty.

Who Owns This Right?
(Who Uses It?)

This one issue: "Who holds and exercises the Right to Nominate?" renders twentieth-century theories about "one party", versus "multi-party" systems moot.

This issue--this one underlying principle--stays the same in all elective governments, whether there are many parties, two, or none.

IN ITS ABSENCE:

The reality is that this principle [i.e., that the Right to Nominate belongs to the people] exists and *always* operates (whether openly; or silently *in absentia). The reality of its existence can be discerned* by examining the results of it being absent or unknown.

In cases of it being absent, this timeless principle, this missing cornerstone of representative government, nevertheless shows its reality in the following ways:

The People as Objects

If the people's Right to Nominate is lost, usurped or stolen, then the people lose some or all of their rightful sovereignty and become Objects of manipulation.

The People Subjected

> If the people do not have the power or means to nominate
> their own candidates, then they must *necessarily* remain
> subjected to the strategies and manipulation of those who
> *do* nominate candidates.

When the people of a republic have lost or been deprived of the
Right to Nominate, then they lose some or all of their sovereignty;
and their government is almost certain to be debased; to be
bastardized into **manipulocrasy** – *"government by those most
skilled at manipulating the public".*

This kind of republic is obviously not what the Framers tried to
design. It is also *not* a republic that can, in the end, survive.

But sadly, it is *what we have become* because of the ever-increasing
effects of our not-in-the-constitution party system. It is where we
are presently mired.

Primary Elections Do Not Solve This Problem

Primaries were a step forward in their time, and still have some
benefit. But they are, in the end, only a partial measure because
everyone in a primary is either a *party member* or self-nominated.
In practice, this is a severely limited menu.

The people of a republic must possess the power and the means,
independent of the government and *independent of all parties,* to
seek out and nominate candidates for public office.

The people must have the power *in their own hands* to nominate
candidates, regardless of whether political parties exist or do not
exist. And they must have this power independent from parties, if
parties do exist.

Without the people's Right to Nominate being constitutionally protected and its exercise provided for by law, our history sadly shows that no republic can come to full maturity, not even ours.

TWO CENTURIES!

Two centuries of experience has shown that an atmosphere of *party strife,* laced with demagoguery, slander, phoniness and manipulation will shove aside Reason and crush Civil Discourse and will inexorably prevail in a republic where the people have no other choices but to choose *between parties.*

THE REMEDY

The people must have in their own hands the independent means to search out and nominate candidates for public office. Only in this way can they provide themselves with **real choice**, an alternative in each and every election, to *parties* and to party candidates.

Once in place this Constitutional balance, this **check** to all parties will forever remain effective no matter how many parties might exist now, disappear or crop up in the future.

Once the people's Right to Nominate is established by Amendment and its exercise is provided for; and when a sufficient number of independent candidates have been drawn by the invitation of their fellow-citizens out of private life into public service (i.e., are citizen-nominated, then elected), then the parties in a leaner, less corrupt, less arrogant, chastened and reduced form can still serve a useful function by defining some issues, initiating debate and providing a few gifted leaders.

But their choke-hold, their complete control over all legislation and over all public expenditures, in violation of the Framers' design and the people's sovereignty, **must come to an end.**

AFTER THAT

Once the people are able to elect whatever numbers they may choose of their own freely nominated candidates, it follows that any influence parties might wield after that will have to be earned. Their influence will no longer be automatic, (no matter what they do); no longer total; no longer able to be casually and easily abused.

They will finally have real competition.

THEN, THE AMERICAN REPUBLIC WILL FINALLY BE FUNCTIONING AS THE FRAMERS ORIGINALLY DESIGNED IT.

Parties will not disappear. In fact, they may improve and do better. They may become much more lean and efficient at *serving* the people, once the people have the means ready at hand to discipline them.

In this way we will put in place the last great cornerstone of representative government.

In this way the Second Omission of the Framers (the lack of a mechanism for the people to nominate their own candidates) will be supplied. [The First Omission was supplied by the Bill of Rights.]

In this way the original design of the American Constitution will be restored and at last become fully operational.

PART V

CHAPTER FOURTEEN

Bad Government

Before we go on to propose a Constitutional mechanism for exercising the Right to Nominate, it's first necessary to understand how severely the parties have trashed the original design of our Republic; and why we must change this dysfunctional form of government.

The parties-only system is not benign; it is ruinous, rapacious. The party system as we have experienced it produces **bad government** in ways that include the following:

ONGOING PLAN, OR GOVERNMENT BY LURCH?

A majority of voters, if they were able to do so, would choose some of the agendas of both parties and combine these into a stable, ongoing plan of government. They cannot do this under the present system.

In practice, the party system makes frustratingly sure that whatever portion of the out-of-power party's agenda that a majority of the voters still want, they will not get.

Voters are forced into a pattern of "government by lurches".

The only discipline voters can exercise is to vote *out* a party from power, even though they still approve of some of this party's practices; and to vote *in* the opposing party, even though they disapprove of some (or much) of *that* party's agenda.

Or the voters can put one party into legislative, and another into executive, power – often producing gridlock (not balance, as the people might have hoped).

The voters simply have no other choices. The result is a only a crude approximation of representative government: "Governing by lurches". The only instrument voters have to correct bad government is to lurch from one party to the other. Then back.

This is crude, and takes a long time. It is purely a product of the parties-only system. It can only continue as long as the parties can maintain a closed system, a system which denies Americans the opportunity to vote for high quality non-party candidates whenever they would like to, or would choose to.

This kind of government by lurches is restrictive and primitive, unfit for a developed nation. As a model, it should have been left behind long ago; and would have been if our Republic had had an unobstructed freedom to mature. But the fierceness of unbridled self-interest, being serviced and locked-in by the party system, has held back our process of maturing.

One inevitable (but strange) result, not often highlighted in civics textbooks, is that *the government is always doing <u>something</u> that the majority of the people don't want it to do.*

In fact, because of built-in party system dysfunction, the government is continually doing things--some of them serious-- that are unwanted by a majority of the people; thus deepening the people's sense of frustration over their lost sovereignty.

HIDDEN AGENDAS

Sadly, it is well within the capability and cunning of those who control parties to utilize their honest members as window-dressing, as cover for their commitments to hidden clients and special interests and to ideological camps representing philosophies the people do not want but which leadership elements are determined to impose on them.

The way parties work at present, there cannot be honest and effective legislation governing interests to whom party leaders have made secret commitments, no matter how much rhetoric or how many promises to "fight for" this or that, which an honest party candidate may have employed during elections. Such promises are mostly empty; as dishonest candidates well know.

Party leaders have become skilled at weakening and watering down regulatory agencies over time, for example, so that financial regulators or drug oversight panels become ineffectual. Such a "window-dressing" agency is worse than no agency at all. These agencies have been rendered into an *appearance* of government, which is only there to placate and manipulate the public.

Such practices are examples of *manipulacracy*. The end result is a debased and hollowed-out republic that does not serve its people.

This is another result of party government, one foreseen by the Framers:

> *"It will rarely happen that the advancement of the public service will be the primary object either of party victories or of party negotiations.*
> *Federalist #76(5)*

There are a number of ongoing but semi-hidden agendas within each of the major parties. The primary hidden agenda tends to be greed and ambition; but in second place comes ideological aggression.

Party Abuses

"Ideological aggression" means the determination to force an ideological model upon the American people which they do not want and have not chosen. The tactic for this kind of party aggression is to run for office based on more popular issues; and then, in office, implement an ideological agenda which was never consciously chosen by the people.

This kind of ideological aggression is degrading to the very *existence* of a republic. It substitutes the judgment of a few for the judgment of the people and uses manipulation to implement that judgment.

A true republic can only flourish if its people develop and maintain enough independent sound judgment to be able to make good evaluations of public policies and of candidates for office.

Not a Full Check

Although political parties compete for votes, history has sternly taught us that parties do not function as a sufficient check on one another.

Parties do present a partial check to each other but not enough to ensure good (or even stable) government. The partial check they offer is unreliable and subject to frequent compromise and shifting principles; and is often based on temporary advantage.

Parties constantly adopt portions of their competitors' agendas in an attempt to lure voters, a practice which at times may have merit.

But the long term effect of that resembles the binary systems found in astronomical bodies, wherein two stars or planets orbit *around each other*, sometimes with enormous gravitational force.

Thomas Peterson

Nonetheless, they are locked together in a grand trajectory and end up whirling off in the same overall direction.

It Doesn't Work As Advertised

The alleged "check" of party toward party does not measure up to what is required at the Constitutional level.

SORRY, BUT THE UGLY REALITY IS…

It's crucial to understand that, in terms of Constitutional issues, parties tend to deepen and make more permanent the divisions in society, not heal them. Party resources, in terms of money and manpower, derive mainly from emphasizing conflict and rarely, if ever, from healing it.

The Framers saw this and other dangers clearly, concluding from their reading of history that the majority of past republics have been *ripped apart* by parties (*aka* factions); have *failed* through abuse of their treasuries; or a combination of both. Others were reduced to paralysis by rabid partisanship, thus becoming useless.

America in the first decades of the 21st century is a long way down this party road to ruin, just as the Framers warned might happen. Whether America *can* recover from the effects of party government and cultural degradation has become an issue in doubt, in the minds of many of our most thoughtful citizens

Money, The Mother's Milk of…Parties

"Politics is about only two things," a party leader once said, "Money, and I forget the other one." Money in politics is not a simple topic. The Framers labored long and hard over the proper role of money and property in a republic. The subject deserves a more complete, separate treatment.

But the purpose right now is to note how far the degradation of our government has progressed under the rule of parties. A cynical joke sums it up: "Americans have the best government that money can buy!"

It is safe to say that the modern party attitude toward money, if placed on a scale and measured by the Framers' way of thinking, would rank at the bottom of that scale. It would rank as a degraded, corrupted form of government alien to what the Framers designed.

You'd have an easier time getting the Framers to accept and put on stinking, filthy wet underwear fished out of a sewer beneath a prison than to accept the present-day party attitude toward money in politics.

Endorsement Abuse

Endorsements have become so routine and expected in party campaigns, that we think little of them. We've almost stopped holding politicians accountable for their bad endorsements.

When a politician announces with great fervor or gravitas that a fellow member of his or her party will make "a great senator/ or governor", when the endorser actually despises that person, considering them incompetent or crooked, then the public's trust is being harmed. This kind of lying has become customary with the parties and is commonly expected.

This is a more serious issue than is normally realized, because it goes to the exploitation of human trust. The human brain is wired in such a way that "two or three witnesses" can serve to "establish" that something is true.

Exploiting this positive human trait by lying may bring a short-term gain. But trust is the foundation of civil government; of the economy (witness what happens when the people of a nation no longer trust their currency); and of civilized society itself.

Party abuse of public trust through phony endorsements is a significant part of public dissatisfaction and anger with our politicians. In the long term, it is a practice that can only be described as heinously stupid and corrosive.

HYPER-CORRUPTION

American politics have become so money-driven, with politicians chasing money and with their campaigns ever more dependent on it, that those elected tend to enter office under heavy obligation to the special interests that *provide* the money.

This leaves most of the people without much hope for honest government done for the good of the whole community. People understand instinctively that money comes with "strings" of expectation, and with invisible obligations.

Any politician—without exception—who claims he or she can accept money without it affecting their judgment on issues is lying. If he truly believes this claim, then he is lying even to himself. He (or she) is self-deluded and should be turned out of office. It is simply not possible for a human being to knowingly *accept money* from a source, and not be affected.

It is possible for someone to accept a donation from a source with whom there is already substantial agreement, and not be *much* affected. In fact, that's how money contributions should be interpreted by voters. Any other claim deserves the closest scrutiny, if not outright scorn.

Recent polls show that a strong majority of voters (67% or more) would favor a 100% turnover of Congress—that all members would be replaced at once, and Congress begun anew. This level of anger and distrust is understandable given government's dysfunction under party rule, but wouldn't it be better to have some criteria to decide by, in order not to kick out the decent with the corrupt?

Voters who are serious about 'turning over' the members of Congress, or even two thirds of Congress, could not find a better indicator to decide who goes than what is offered by the common saying, "follow the money". If a legislator talks one way but votes another, "follow the money".

If the banking system collapses and citizens want to find who's politically responsible, they need only count up all the votes taken over time affecting that industry; then add up political contributions, and "follow the money".

The same guideline holds for the drug industry: count up all votes over time, then add up contributions and "follow the money". The same applies to other interest groups.

In fact, "Follow the Money" citizen committees could provide a great service to the country by helping voters understand who to turn out of office, and why.

Access

Party money-brokering has gone so far that it is not uncommon for campaign staffers or friends of some lawmakers to request large donations of money from citizen groups with the understanding that those groups will then have access to the lawmaker.

Buying access is corrupt. Both seller and buyer have undermined republican government.

But old-fashioned corruption has largely been replaced in these instances by a far more sophisticated *"hyper-corruption"* in which nothing is ever said that could be repeated as evidence in court of a "quid pro quo" ("this for that").

No more of the old-fashioned method: cash in an envelope in exchange for a vote (except in Chicago and some other places where there is great reverence for party traditions).

But even in Chicago, a level of sophistication has developed in some circles almost worthy of the CIA, in that not only do crooks know to never leave a paper trail nor write emails; they know not even to *speak* of crooked deals except in the rarest, most controlled circumstances. This tactic could have been learned from the Mafia. It comes with the assumption that there may be recording devices anywhere.

SPIN

It's possible to convey a false impression of events without saying anything that can be proven to contradict known facts. Just leave selected parts out of the account, and it sounds totally different from what actually happened. Or just emphasize some facts, and make others sound insignificant: the hearers will be given a false impression of the event.

There is an ancient name for misrepresenting reality: Lying.

In recent times, political lying has begun to be called "spin". There is nothing new about spin—it's as old as the human race. In prehistory, humans began requiring oaths to be taken at trials, in an effort to forestall lying. Our Anglo-American oath has good reason for its wording: "Do you solemnly swear *to tell the truth, the whole truth, and nothing but the truth?*"

If employees lie about cash flow, quality control or customer satisfaction, a business can be quickly destroyed.

But "spinning" by politicians has come to be treated like a competitive sport in our media.

A republic, more than any other form of government, depends upon a steady supply of truth being available to the people. "Spin" should be met harshly in a republic, with rejection from public office through election defeat or impeachment.

Tolerating "spin" would be insane in business, sports, the military, construction, or any other worthwhile effort. But **party politics** is full of it; it has even been warping some of our government agencies and their statistics. Names attached to bills in Congress have become ridiculous in some cases for their manipulative "spin", making these bills sound entirely different from what they really are.

Do these manipulators really think people are that stupid? Obviously, they do. Just as obviously, such people—the lying *manipulocrats* of the party system--should be turned out of office as quickly as possible when the people have their right to Nominate restored.

Spin will continue to get worse until the people can smack it down to a minimum by voting both parties out at the same time.

"Spinners are liars" should be a voter's motto.

Nothing is likely to draw a clearer line between respected nominees, people of integrity from private life, *versus* party candidates in future elections than the parties' incessant use of lying "spin". It sometimes seems like all they know.

SLURP

Because the parties have gotten where they are by usurping much of the rightful sovereignty of the people (quietly transforming the people's representatives into *their* representatives) perhaps they should make some additions to their playbook of advice to newly elected party members.

Along with maxims like "You gotta go along to get along," and "Remember to dance with them that brung ya," they should add, with a wink, "We had to usurp, to slurp," to infuse a party interpretation of history into new officeholders.

If anyone thinks this characterization too harsh, he or she need only review the history of "pork" and "earmarks" from both parties then ponder the meaning of a 19 TRILLION dollar debt.

But behind the debt lurks a much uglier monster that must be faced: the ***helplessness of the people to stop*** any of these practices.

The people's helplessness to stop party fiscal abuse is **PROOF OF WHERE SOVEREIGNTY LIES TODAY.**

This is not "government of the people". The people hate these things!

Party leaders have long known this and factored it into their calculations. They know that voters are angry and frustrated but they tend to think that they can find ways to *turn that anger* against the other party, and thus capitalize on it. So they continue in the same nation-destroying game at which they have developed so much skill. They've learned...that the people can't stop them.

FREEDOM! (FROM PARTY DOMINATION)

What party leaders have *not* calculated is what will happen to them when the voters are finally free to vote for outstanding non-party candidates, over and over, in every election. And so become able to (finally!) *get rid* of the worst liars, the spinners, the negative-ad perps; and the "go along to get along" money wasters in *both* parties.

Getting rid of odious politicians will be deeply gratifying to Americans, an extended feast. It will be a celebration that could last for years, perhaps a decade or more after adopting the Right to Nominate amendment.

But it will not satisfy us forever.

Americans long to be able to vote in a positive way that will be productive; that will bring real results to genuinely improve our nation's life. *That* will be the end result of the Right to Nominate.

WHO TO KICK OUT:

When Americans realize that having the Right to Nominate restored can break the strongholds of selfishness that rule their country through the party system, through both parties, then they will choose to get that Right back. And they will kick out of office any and every politician who tries to keep that Right from them or who tries to delay or hinder it.

And when they find that after electing a minimum number of *their own representatives* that the insolent, overweening power of the parties is broken, that the balance of power is returning to the people and that the parties now have to come to them--to <u>their</u> representatives--in order to do anything, then the people will sense the beginning return of their long lost sovereignty.

Americans will rejoice when the Constitution's design is restored and "...government of the people, by the people, and for the people" returns to its native land.

RESTORATION, NOT MERE REFORM

It is important to note here that this book deals with *restoration* of the Constitutional design, not with a myriad of issues which might call for reform. Understandably this might disappoint reformers.

The reason for pointing out the excesses and corruptions of party-only government in this book is not to reform the party system.

Reforms tend to last only a few election cycles because of the adaptability and ferocious appetites of the parties. So reforms must be done and redone to maintain civic health; but they are not the focus of this book.

WHY WE MUST CHANGE OUR PRESENT FORM OF GOVERNMENT

Trying to reform the present party system is useless. It was corrupt and slanderous at its birth. Lying, malice and fierce rivalry are embedded deep in party DNA.

The parties-only system is contrary to our Constitution; it is dead-set against the Framers' design. Trying to reform the parties-only system would be like throwing handfuls of straw at a charging rhinoceros.

Only the application of power, operating through our votes, can put an end to the parties-only system. And the power which is supposed to be in the people's votes (but today isn't) can only be restored when their Right to Nominate is secured constitutionally.

Parties will always be around in some form.

But parties-*only* in control, as a regime, as a form of government, **must be abolished.**

> *"Whenever any form of government becomes destructive of these ends, it is the right of the people to alter or abolish it..."*
> *-The Declaration of Independence*

Such words should never be uttered lightly or merely as heated rhetoric. Their first utterance triggered six years of war.

But we can no longer avoid or put off a decision. If we fail to make this decision history will make it for us. We are nineteen *TRILLION dollars* in debt as of early 2016.

And the sovereignty of the people has been so drained away, so weakened, by the parties-only system, that we as a nation *cannot stop* our politicians from financially ruining us. How pathetic is that?

This is not "government of the people".

We must take the sober decision to *change* this form of government.

This decision should be made deliberately, just as the Founding generation deliberated before adopting the Constitution

Our American experiment in government has gone on long enough to reach at least one conclusion: No republic can survive—or thrive--unless its Constitution gives its people the *upper hand over all parties.*

Which is exactly how the Framers designed our system to work.

The problem we face is timeless. Any future free republics, should they spring up, will have parties in them. The parties will compete.

If those parties gain total control of government then these future republics will be destroyed just as has happened in the past and is happening now.

Destructive To Liberty

The parties-only system is destructive to our liberty at the nomination stage of elections.

Liberty must be restored to the nominating phase of our elections. Until it is, we won't have the government the Framers designed; we won't have a true or mature republic.

We won't have "…government of the people, by the people, and for the people".

We'll be stuck instead with "…*government **of** the parties, **by** the parties, and **for** the parties' clients and special interests.*"

We

If "We the people" are going to regain our function as The Boss by putting power back into our votes, then we need to be realistic. Realism requires that every American take a good hard look at our politics, and at their results, and ask, "Do I want it to go on like this?"

If not, then the only way to stop this headlong course of political tragedy is to put a **stop** to the parties-only regime.

To repeat what must remain obvious, this does not mean that parties or their freedom to do what they lawfully choose should be stopped.

No, we must stop the abysmal **un**-checked, **un**-balanced liberty-restricting election system which gives up without a whimper and hands complete control over our nominations and our government, again and again, to the parties.

THIS GENERATION

This generation of Americans faces an historic assignment, an unavoidable "rendezvous with destiny", to echo F.D.R.'s fateful words to the World War II generation.

Our generation must find an answer to the timeless dilemma presented by political parties. This dilemma has been unresolved for over 2,600 years:
What must a republic do about parties, to survive?

We must determine what role parties may play in our free government and how and where they must be checked.

Parties-**only** in control, as a form of government, must be **put away forever** to resolve this historic dilemma. The people, through their representatives, must be put back in control and their rightful sovereignty restored.

The Timeless Work

Parties will always exist. Our job--the job of the generation now living--is to do what has never been done before: to *bring political parties to heel,* to make them SERVE "We the people" instead of fleecing, lying to, dividing and manipulating them.

That will be a watershed in human history, one that not even our Founders could quite accomplish (though they came very close, closer than any before them).

The great foundation they laid has made it possible for this generation to step in and complete their work.

PART VI

CHAPTER FIFTEEN

How?

The question that arises once we have the principle fixed firmly in our minds --that the Right to Nominate belongs to the people--is this:

How can we set up a mechanism for the people to exercise this Right in an open and fair way? How can we devise a mechanism which will not become subject to manipulation and corruption like the party system?

To lay the foundation for our approach to this question, we must turn to the Framers for their approach toward the design of government.

Their approach was practical as well as philosophical. It was a way of thinking they largely shared and was put into words by John Dickenson, a delegate from Pennsylvania, who stood up at the Convention and said:

"Experience is a better guide than Reason."

The notion that the Federal Convention of 1787 was a sort of giant brainstorming session where all sorts of new ideas were batted around and somehow from this whirling mix the delegates invented a new government is absurd and wrong.

Like successful men in any field they adhered strongly to forms that had already been tested and proven through experience. They were flexible and open enough to be willing to hear new ideas, without which they could not have succeeded. But after hearing ideas they immediately began to put them to a practical test: Had such an arrangement, or something close to it, been tried before? How did it work out in practice? What were the reasons for its failure or success? Could the reasons for success be applied in different circumstances? And so on.

So they were open to innovative ideas but thought that these should have some way of being tested by historical comparisons. They were, in short, analyzing history; weeding out causes of failure in governments and grafting in elements of success. Like political architects, and like builders, they worked first with the blueprints and plans; then with the "timbers and stones" of governmental realities throughout known history, especially as those realities had been encountered under the British constitution.

This approach of the Framers--the practical application of historical experience--must be ours as well, even as we consider something that may at first appear to be new: How do we construct a Constitutional mechanism for exercising the people's Right to Nominate?

In reality, such a mechanism should not and would not contain anything new. It should be put together out of well-tried, tested elements. It is only the *configuration* of these elements that should be new.

HISTORICAL MODELS

The two most effective historical models for us to consider in designing a mechanism for the people to exercise their Right to Nominate are the Jury and the Convention. Both are tried and proven. If we take the best elements from each and merge them we will have formed an almost perfect vehicle for citizen nominations.

TWO ELEMENTS OF A
NOMINATING BODY:

THE JURY AND THE CONVENTION

The best features of these two historic, successful institutions, the Jury and the Convention, should be combined as a vehicle for citizen nominations.

Before such a Nominating Body would convene, steps of preparation would have to be taken.

First Steps

In Preparation: In advance of each election an independent, non-political board appointed by each state will by mail solicit every registered voter for the name of a person with whom they have had personal experience, whom they respect; and whom they think would make a good candidate for public office.

The form sent to each voter should be a simple single-page legal document, to be signed and warranted to contain true information under penalty of perjury.

Clear guidelines (and prohibitions) must be explained in regard to this document. Nominations are voluntary. There is no obligation involved. However, if making a nomination is the voter's choice, then basic guidelines must apply: No one may nominate a relative; an employer or fellow employee; or anyone having a financial connection or obligation to the voter.

Any mentoring relationship (teacher, spiritual leader, therapist, legal advisor, etc.) must have been inactive for at least 4 years before the nomination of that person may be offered.

Any public figure *not personally known* by the voter would be *ineligible* for that voter's nomination at this stage. Public figures from the world of sports and entertainment would be ineligible, period. Such persons would have an unfair advantage; and the source of their popularity would seriously debase the political process.

Such persons would have an open road before them to run for office with a party (if they want to run and have something of substance to offer), so this exclusion takes nothing from their rights. But let such a candidacy depend on its substance, not on empty entertainment fame.

Demagoguery and public relations efforts are enemies to this process.

P.R. DISQUALIFIES

The basic idea is to draw upon the personal knowledge and experience of private citizens gained during the normal course of their lives. Any hint of a public relations effort must **disqualify** a potential nominee. Nominating Juries would be so instructed by law.

To benefit the Republic, the public nominating process must exclude any hint of "celebrity-ism," a bankrupt and degraded spirit which is antithetical to republican values. Anyone still engaged in "celebrity worship" is mentally and emotionally too immature to vote. Politicians who promote celebrity adulation degrade a republic's political process and should be removed from office. Such activity should be recognized in law as grounds for impeachment.

Necessary Questions

The voter should be asked several direct questions: How well do you know the person you are nominating? How much interaction have you had with him or her, and what was the nature of it? The voter then would be asked, "What drew your attention and respect to this person, to the extent you would nominate them for public office?"

To safeguard the process, very specific questions must be asked: Has anyone suggested that you nominate this person? Has anyone spoken to you to promote this person's nomination? If so, who? Have you ever participated in an effort to influence legislation? If so, is this nomination related to that effort in any way? Has anyone offered <u>anything</u> to induce you to nominate? Do you swear/affirm that this nomination is yours alone, and not induced by others? And so on.

These questions, and others, are necessary to prevent the citizen nomination process from being subverted to the purposes of activists or organized groups--a course that would end up reproducing the same steps which gave rise to political parties in the first place.

Further safeguards will be needed and discussed later but these all will have the same objective: to produce a "clean" list of nominees who have earned the genuine respect of their neighbors and fellow citizens, and whose names are not generated by activists or by any organized campaign.

These required questions, answered under oath, are intended to give a nominating Jury/Convention the basic information it will need in order to sift through the names submitted en route to making a final selection of public Nominees.

When all steps of preparation are accomplished and a list of freely offered names has been compiled from the voters, the Nominating Jury is convened.

The list of names submitted is likely to fall into a statistical pattern: a high number of single-digit mentions; and a much lower concentration of names mentioned by multiple voters. The Jury will have to ascertain why some names show up many times but if the reasons are spontaneous (not the result of a campaign) and wholly legitimate, this fact can aid in the Jury's search.

The independent Office responsible for soliciting voter nominations must include an investigative staff. When the Nominating Body has narrowed the list of names submitted down to a manageable number (say, ten to twenty) these investigators act immediately to verify that each nomination remaining was made in good faith and in accordance with law and that no organized campaign or undue influence was involved.

At this point, the list of names is released to the public, without comment. The public and all media are encouraged to make known any hidden campaign or behind-the-scenes influence which might be attached to any of these potential nominees, to help augment and complete the vetting process.

ELEMENT ONE:
THE JURY

The Jury is large, ranging in size from thirty to one hundred-twenty members, depending on each state's choice. Like all juries, its members are chosen by random selection from the full registry of voters.

During the second half of its deliberations, the Jury will switch to Convention mode, with all of its proceedings open to the public.

The Jury model must be the heart of this Jury/Convention hybrid; while the Convention model supplies its open-to-the-public operating mode during the second half of deliberations.

But in its ultimate act, the vote to nominate final candidates, the nominating body meets first in Jury form, but *in public view,* in order to remind its members of their oath to perform a public duty. Then their final vote, taken as a Convention, will also be open to public view.

But: Is There a Problem?

If the Jury and the Convention embody the best historical models for exercising the people's Right to Nominate, won't we have a potential problem?

Who chooses the jury?

Who decides who gets to go to this hybrid Convention?

WHO APPOINTS THEM?

Jury/Convention appointment must be done by a process of random selection for the following reasons:

First, there is no process by which an appointed committee or panel could select a Jury of nominators without the prejudices and interests of the panel members influencing their selections.

Who would appoint the members of such a panel, a panel to select another panel? Wouldn't that first panel become, or at least be seen as, the new equivalent of the old back-room nominee pickers?

Even the most well-intended selection process, if done by human beings, would be highly vulnerable to the perception of bias and unfairness.

SOMETHING NEW:

We do have something the Framers did not have: the discovery in mathematics of the laws of probability which govern statistical chance (or random selection). These laws have proven so reliable that billions of dollars are staked annually on their consistent operation.

Polling done well (according to the laws of probability) has proven so reliable that a margin of error of only three or four percentage points (in a representative sample of about 1000) has become the norm. For this reason, candidates and political parties pay millions of dollars to obtain these polls and form their election strategies according to them.

But even though the scientific description of these laws is recent, their existence is not. They've always been present and always have worked. Humans have long sensed their existence and used them successfully.

Many different cultures throughout history have drawn lots to settle disputes. Even more important, people have drawn lots to settle *potential* disputes. Many a college student has arrived on campus to begin the school year and upon arrival found out what dorm room he has been awarded by a random drawing. This process is instinctively (and correctly) perceived as fair and unbiased.

When a military draft was in effect during the Vietnam era, young men were drafted through random selection of numbers representing days of the year--birthdays. Even with lives and futures on the line and controversy in the air this method of selection was universally perceived as unbiased.

It turns out, of course, that these perceptions about unbiased decisions were correct, having been solidly based in mathematical science even during the centuries before the science was known.

NOW, THE SCIENCE IS KNOWN

But because this science is now well known we can be sure beyond any doubt that a completely fair method of selection for a nominating body (the Jury/Convention), free from cronyism, from corruption, from undue influence or manipulation of any kind, is available to us.

The random selection of a certain number of voters, taken from the full registry in a particular state to serve on a nominating Jury/Convention, will provide as close a representation of the opinions and attitudes of all the voters in that state as is humanly possible.

Because random selection does represent the general population accurately, there will be a tiny percentage of mentally unstable people--perhaps only one or two--included in the initial selections. The Jury/Convention must have the power and the legal charge to quickly remove any disruptive or mentally incapacitated person at any point in its deliberations.

No committee, no blue-ribbon panel, even with the best intentions and the most exhaustive list of qualifications could ever equal this result, in terms of a highly accurate cross-section that faithfully represents the opinions and attitudes of the voting population.

The random selection of a Nominating Body *must* be done by physical, publicly observable means, available for examination at any time. This process should never be electronic, in order to merit the trust of the people.

The Jury: Trust Earned

The Jury has for centuries been a bastion protecting the rights and liberties of the English-speaking world. A major tenet of the Magna Charta, signed in 1215, which protected the rights of Englishmen against arbitrary use of power by kings, contained a provision for the right to trial by jury and that jury had to be composed of one's peers.

For centuries the most difficult decisions impacting private citizens have been entrusted to juries: guilt or innocence of crime, life or death, awards for damages. Grand juries have been entrusted with investigative powers to determine cause for criminal prosecution.

Juries are not perfect. They are composed of human beings. They work best with careful and impartial instructions on how to apply law. But their record of sound decisions reached through earnest labor is far better than the cumulative records of most legislatures, bureaucracies and executive departments of government.

What has made juries work so well over many centuries? Why have these panels of ordinary citizens, though imperfect, become one of the most trusted and essential components of our way of life?

Commitment By Choice

At the core of jury effectiveness lays the reality of a commitment to public duty, as undertaken by free people. When free men or women first choose and then pledge to accept a duty or a public responsibility and carry it out to the best of their ability the result can become one of the strongest and purest motivations for positive public labor the world has ever known.

The American military, as one example, is presently one of the finest in history because it is comprised of free men and women who *choose* to make a commitment to duty. This has produced a powerful combination: strong dedication and work ethic plus a level of flexibility which slavish, conscripted, top-down militaries can never attain.

The Jury model has worked well because of the presence of three primary elements: 1. A free people who freely *choose to commit* themselves to performing a public duty. 2. A noble and necessary ideal which is explicitly set before them (to "do justice" or "protect and defend"). 3. An oath or affirmation is made and a charge is accepted.

When these three elements are put in place, then everything depends on these "ordinary" persons being motivated from within to do as they have said. Our justice system then depends on them, our military and police, and so on. This commitment and "carry-through" are at the heart of how free people exercise self-government. Surprisingly often, this system produces the highest quality of justice and service seen in human history.

Freedom works. It is the gift of God and the intended state of man. A freely chosen commitment made by a free man or woman is one of the most powerful forces on earth. In terms of reliability and durability (among other things), few other motives can compare.

This reality lies at the core of the Jury system and would form the very heart of the Jury/Convention nominating body.

Responsibility

Jurors who serve on criminal cases are quickly sobered by their responsibility. Flippancy or shallow opinions about "What ought to be done to criminals!" have to be discarded.

In a similar way, being politically opinionated, irresponsible, or party-infected would all have to be set aside by oath and by charge for those serving on a Jury/Convention. This is particularly important in the search phase which is the first half of the Jury's work.

Responsibility and commitment are sobering.

The words of an oath or affirmation, if well crafted, can serve to summarize a citizen's commitment, whether to military duty, government office or jury service. If this oath is coupled with a charge (also freely accepted) then the power of commitment becomes accurately focused and very effective.

When normal citizens accept the responsibility of jury service in a criminal or civil case, they accept a charge to *do justice* toward the people involved, to the best of their ability. It has long been a source of satisfaction, and sometimes amazement, on the part of judges and lawyers to see how seriously most jurors take their duty and how hard they try to "get it right."

THE HYBRID

A Nominating Jury will necessarily be larger than a normal jury--often between 30 and 120 members--and must conduct many of its operations openly under clear rules of order on the model of a Convention. Whether operating in Jury or Convention mode, the nominating body would normally make decisions by majority vote.

The heart of this hybrid model will continue to be drawn from the Jury--the acceptance of a public duty by free people with a commitment to carry that duty out to the best of the jurors' abilities--confirmed by oath or affirmation and accompanied by clear and impartial instructions on how to do the task.

These historically proven elements will insure that the Jury/ Convention will work.

INSTRUCTIONS TO THE JURY

The instructions given the Jury to do its work must include setting aside any partisan considerations during the initial *search* phase, which is solely dedicated to finding a list of defined characteristics in possible nominees.

These characteristics should be basic and straightforward: a record of honesty and proven ability, a history of integrity, decent and civil treatment of others, good sense and sound judgment, and above all, the genuine respect of their neighbors and fellow citizens.

Ability and Virtue

The criteria for high public office—especially the presidency-- named by the Framers were simple: Ability and Virtue.[27]

"Virtue" in the 1700's was a word which included the signal elements of what we today call "character." In the Framers' worldview, Virtue (excellent character) was ideally a prerequisite to public office. But being realists, they deliberately created a design which would continue to function in spite of persons of low or bad character occasionally holding office.

Their design did not, however, anticipate a government locked under the control of parties, which would bring in a flood of cronyism and much-lowered standards of character.

PHASE ONE:
The Search For Qualifications

The impartial instructions given the Nominating Jury for its initial *search* phase should be focused on defined characteristics. During

---

[27] *Federalist #68, (8)*

this phase no examinations would be held as to partisan-influenced positions on public issues.

Defined character qualities are the sole objective in this phase.

Only later, once a pool of nominees of good character is established, should the assessment of understanding and good judgment on issues important to the public be tackled.

It is clear, however, that even in this first phase of inquiry the Jury/Convention members would have to be making judgment calls just to narrow their list down to a manageable number.

Making those kind of judgments to the best of their ability is what a jury or convention is supposed to do as part of their job definition.

During Phase One, the search phase, only citizens who give their consent would be considered. Some of the Jury's work in this first phase will have to take place in closed session. There will occasionally be some review of 'derogatory information' and the privacy of those citizens who consent to be considered in this phase needs to be assured.

THE NOMINATING BODY

ELEMENT #TWO:
CONVENTION

The initial search phase requires privacy because it will include quietly dropping candidates with a flawed record and eliminating those obviously unsuitable or whose name-submission process contained questionable elements. The object is *to identify those with the most outstanding positive qualities* so that the list of candidates is narrowed down to a manageable number.

Then personal interviews between these finalist candidates and the Jury/Convention would begin.

During this phase the Nominating body changes mode to operate in the form of a Convention. All further proceedings should be open for viewing by the public.

But little or no input *from* the public should be allowed in order to prevent a circus atmosphere or partisan interference or any attempts at manipulation from without. The public could follow, through broadcast outlets, the whole course of interviewing: the questions asked; the answers given by potential Nominees and all comments from Jury/Convention members.

During this stage, which would lead up to voting for final Nominees, any questions, any topics, any issues (partisan or not) important to Jury/ Convention members should be permitted.

All members of the Jury/Convention should have an allotted number of minutes—if they choose to use them--to say whatever they want prior to voting. When that time is up they must stop speaking. Period. Rules of order are strictly enforced. No disruptions are allowed. Decisions are made by majority vote.

These interviews, these Civil Dialogues, will obviously weigh heavily in the Jury/Convention's decisions, as will the comments and views of fellow members of the Jury.

A Clear Charge, A Final Decision

But in the end, the members of the Jury/Convention will simply have to use their best judgment to make final choices; which is exactly what every jury must do; and exactly what their oath and their charge would state:

"From among those recommended by the people,
seek out and nominate the best candidates
for public office you can find."

Simple and clear.

By majority vote -- after vetting, interviewing, and engaging in real
civil discourse -- final choices are made in full public view.

Non-party public candidates will at this point be nominated;
chosen by a Body which is a representative cross-section of
the community. Chosen from among highly respected citizens
recommended by the people themselves.

These **non**-party nominees will be put on the ballot for the general
election.

The Uplifting Power
Of Honest Public Discourse

Central to the Jury/Convention's interviews of potential nominees
is the reality, already established, that those being interviewed
are among the must honorable and respected citizens in the
community. The atmosphere, therefore, of the interviews should
always be respectful, honest and straightforward. The instructions
given the Jury should be very clear in this regard.

The most difficult questions can and should be asked; but with
the purpose of eliciting the honest thought processes of our most
respected citizens. Never is the purpose to "grill" them.

How have these citizens, who have gained such respect from their
neighbors, wrestled with, or thought through, difficult issues?
What perspectives do they bring to issues which challenge us all?

The very practice of hearing the earnest thoughts of respected fellow citizens as part of the lead-up to every election can, and will, uplift our entire political process.

This is especially true since these thoughts will come not as mere discussion but will come from citizens for whom Americans can then choose to _vote_.

The value of honest, civil discourse in a republic cannot be overstated

BUT, IN CONTRAST

Voters are sick to death of the canned, dumbed-down "talking points" approach of the parties. This party approach is an insult to the intelligence of caring voters. It is aimed at voters who "aren't paying attention." But even they are sick of it; it probably has the effect that they will pay even less attention.

There is a veritable avalanche of anger and frustration built up in the minds of American voters toward politicians. When Americans wake up to the fact that after their Right to Nominate is restored, they will *no longer* have to put up with party politicians (except for the few they consider worthy); or with garbage-filled party campaigns; then they *won't* put up with them any more!

That avalanche of anger will descend with a roar to bury the stinking landfills and toxic dumps of party campaigns, which will come to be remembered with regret as part of a primitive, incredibly abusive, tainted and criminal pattern of the past; just as we now look back with regret at the heedless abuse in our past of the natural environment.

Americans long to vote for something truly positive and nation-building. We long for our votes to count again. We sorely miss the rightful sovereignty of "we, the people", which we sense is mostly gone. And we long for the chance to restore our country, to bring it back from degradation and from the brink of catastrophe.

Up-building and Positive

Normal Jury duty is vital to a free society. But it can sometimes be burdensome if it involves difficult cases or sordid crimes.

But service on a Nominating Jury, a Jury/Convention, would be completely different: it would be an opportunity to serve one's community in an extremely positive way.

This jury would be engaging in honest dialogue with the most respected people in our communities about issues which matter to us all.

This Jury would be providing the community with honest and thoughtful civil discourse to replace the debased, often vicious and slanderous campaigns which presently rule our public forum.

To serve on this Jury would bring opportunity for respectful, candid public interchange;--something no healthy republic can do without.

This Jury service, with every convening, would build up the community and steadily improve the quality of government. To serve on such a Jury would be an honor and a pleasure for many Americans, an opportunity for doing good to your country and to your neighbors.

Is There Any Doubt?

Can anyone doubt whether a large Jury, composed of voters, and:

1)having a composition which reflects the community,

2) being well instructed in the requirements of the law,
3) being under oath to perform this duty as a service to the community, to the best of their ability,
4) supplied with needed investigative power (i.e., investigators who work for them, to vet nominees) would:

be perfectly able to cull through a list of potential nominees and after extensive interviews *select by majority vote* a few outstanding individuals (already recommended by fellow citizens), whom they find would make excellent candidates for public office?

The nominees chosen by these independent Jury/Conventions would be placed on the ballot, thus becoming *available* (along with party- or self-nominated candidates) for a choice to be made by all voters in the general election.

If the general public happens to disagree with a particular nomination by a Jury/Convention; or if circumstances change between nomination time and election time, voters will make their final decision accordingly, as they always have. But now voters will have a vetted, respected **non-party alternative** in every general election.

Funding

By law, campaign funds must be provided for these public Nominees. A good rule of thumb would be to match the average spent by major candidates in the previous election for the same office.

The Campaign

Public Nominees would be well advised to hire advisors and to present themselves simply, with dignity and honesty, during the election campaign period.

AT LAST!

If the parties choose to use slanderous, negative tactics against such citizen candidates, then *at last* the voters will be enabled to *get rid of* the negative slander, the vicious attacks and much of the lying phoniness and manipulation of party "campaigns" by *voting such party politicians out*--weeding them out--over and over until their numbers in the government are so reduced that they are forced to stop these tactics or disappear.

"We must take men as we find them."
(attributed to) James Madison

Only when the people can apply the overwhelming power of their votes to say to the parties, "**WE DON'T NEED YOU** ANY MORE!! Get your negative attack-ads off our screens!! Get your slander **OUT OF OUR FACES!**" will the parties be forced to give up these vile practices.

The parties do it under the present system because it works. Only when it doesn't work any more will they stop.

Only when the people are set free to vote *both* parties out, instead of being forced to bounce back and forth between them like a pathetic, kitten-like, powerless captive audience, will the parties listen.

When the people begin to sense their "new" power (which is not new at all but was how the Framers originally designed it), and begin to apply it (through their votes) by getting rid of offenders and putting in accomplished persons from private life will we be able to discipline all party politicians.

At the absolute minimum, and as a baseline, we will *at last* be able to establish civil discourse in our elections.

AND HOW DO WE FIND THEM?

"How we find them" over the course of two hundred years is this: Men who gravitate toward governmental power, who are motivated to seek it, will go farther and farther to grasp after and keep it until they hit an immovable barrier.

We find that such men ultimately stop only when forced to stop. That is the reality behind our Constitutional system of checks and balances.

Internationally, this means that force of arms alone can stop the worst of them. Domestically, it means that party abuses will only get worse and worse until the people are able to **force** them to stop.

We can be thankful that our Constitutional system enables that "stopping power" to be located in our votes, not in the force of arms.

LET'S ASK:

In considering the case for citizen Nominating bodies (i.e., Jury/ Conventions), we should ask ourselves questions like these:

Are normal people too stupid or venal to nominate candidates for public office? (If so, why do they serve so well on civil and criminal juries?)

Are only *party* members able to pick good candidates?

Should only party members be eligible for nomination?

Should only party "professionals" be allowed to touch the hidden lever of power, the power to nominate?

Or does the Right to Nominate, the hidden lever of power, truly belong to the people? Shouldn't the people be able to nominate candidates they've personally experienced during the course of their life, persons they have genuinely come to respect? Candidates many of their fellow citizens would truly want to vote for?

Wouldn't it be true that anyone who thinks the people *unfit* to nominate candidates does not believe in republican government at all?

REMINDER:

While considering such questions, it is vital to remember that primary elections do not solve the problem. Why? Because everyone in a primary is either a party member or self-nominated.

In this sense, the outcome of a primary is rigged.

Not rigged in favor of one party candidate over another. But rigged in the sense that the outcome of party-organized primaries will always be: party candidates!

Voters may be bamboozled over and over by the excitement of a "horse race" into thinking that we have real freedom of choice.

But in reality, the only choice we normally have is either one party pol, or another.

That must end, or it will end our Republic.

STATE BY STATE

In fashioning the statutes governing Jury/Conventions; and in drafting the Instructions that will guide their deliberations, each state will find it necessary to safeguard the process against demagoguery or any attempts to "game" the nominating process.

To meet the Framers' design specs, any proposed change in government structure would have to include strong barriers, difficult or impossible to be breached, against demagoguery.

THINGS TO LEARN

Some states may find it useful to define who is already a "public person" and therefore ineligible (as are entertainment figures) for citizen nomination

Each state will probably find some unique features to add to the effectiveness of its Jury/Conventions. Some states may choose to ask each Jury/Convention to elect one of their number to serve as chairperson for the next Jury. This would assure more continuity over time and less opportunity for confusion.

All States will likely discover that some personalities find great satisfaction in promoting others to occupy positions of influence.

Their motives may range from a "busybody" mindset (seeking to enhance their own self-importance) all the way to a love of community and a genuine intention to do good. As long as their activities are fully disclosed on nomination papers and a record is kept of their activities over time it will simply be up to the Jury to determine whether their efforts have value or not.

As those experienced in public affairs will quickly recognize, after a few election cycles many states will have on hand a small "stable" of unelected public nominees as well as a larger number of elected ones. This will be all to the good. These persons will be able to comment intelligently on public issues from a respected position. The voters may come to wish they had elected such a candidate, who could be re-nominated if the next Jury/Convention were so inclined.

Each state must decide whether or not to allow re-nominations. In either case our civil discourse will be much enriched by having these respected voices available between election cycles.

This will mark a refreshing change toward a culture of ongoing Civil Discourse and away from the people being treated like a mute, childlike captive audience being served up for professional manipulators to "work".

Candidacy through Earned Respect

The public nomination process is designed to seek out candidates who are *proven in life* through their honest conduct and respectful treatment of fellow citizens; through an earned reputation for good judgment, fairness and ability.

Public candidates must be people who have earned by their conduct in the course of business, agriculture, education, civic projects or any other field of real-life endeavor the respect and trust of their neighbors.

PART VII

THE AMENDMENT

The right to nominate candidates for elective office belongs to the people.

The government of [U.S. or State] shall protect and defend this Right; and shall provide such means as are necessary for its orderly exercise, including funds sufficient to promote the candidacies of resulting public nominees, based on the cost of past elections. But government shall not pay expenses incurred by any private group in the course of that group seeking or promoting its own candidates.

SUPPORTIVE CLAUSES
& ENABLING LEGISLATION

a. The States shall have power to determine who will be eligible for public nomination within their jurisdictions; and power to regulate the procedures of nominating Bodies (hereafter referred to as "Jury/Conventions"), provided that said regulations include and comply with the following:

1. Sufficiently prior to each election, registered voters shall be solicited for nominations to the offices to be elected.

2. Those names which are returned, along with supporting comments and reasons given, shall be turned over to a Jury/ Convention of citizens drawn by random selection from the

*full registry of that state's voters who shall have been given
and shall have accepted a solemn duty to seek and find
Candidates for office who, in their best judgment, would well
represent and serve the people of [x districts] in [y offices].*

*3. After hearing from possible candidates invited to
address them, and to hold discussions with them, the
Jury/Convention shall by majority vote nominate a final
candidate or candidates of their choice; whose names shall
then appear on the ballot of the general election, with all
other lawfully nominated candidates.*

*4. The [State legislature] shall establish an Independent
Bureau of Service with the means and personnel to conduct
background investigations of potential nominees. This
Service Bureau shall introduce and explain to each new Jury/
Convention the previous history and required procedures of
the Jury/Convention, according to a format set forth in law.*

*5.) When final Nominees are chosen, this Bureau of Service
will provide them with needed preparation for an election
campaign, including balanced and expert testimony about
issues currently facing the government, and shall at once
supply them with all campaign funds appropriated by [the
legislature].*

*6.) The Bureau's meetings, decisions, and actions shall
be open to public view during this period of preparing
Nominees.*

*The function of this Bureau shall be to serve the Jury/
Convention in whatever manner is required to fulfill its
duty. The Bureau shall help prepare final Nominees for their
election campaigns; but beginning at the campaign's starting
date, as prescribed by law, the Bureau may give no further
aid or advice to any Nominee.*

CHAPTER SIXTEEN

How To Keep a Republic Healthy

1.) Consistently find candidates for public office who are proven in life, and respected; who have shown honesty, ability and good character in private life.

2.) Make advancement in public office depend upon the demonstration of these qualities, plus two more: integrity and sufficient wisdom (insight) to handle various government matters well.

THIS WAS IT.

This was the unwritten system of selection for office experienced by the Framers, which in several stages brought each of them to the Philadelphia Convention; and which they tried to incorporate into the Constitution.

This is the kind of Republic envisioned and hoped for, labored and fought for by the Founding generation.

They did not risk "their lives, their fortunes, and their sacred honor" merely to provide a circus arena for egotists, opportunists, attention seekers and spin-artists to hustle the public for an office.

They did not fight a grueling, dangerous war merely to enable ruthless men, ideologues, or greedy hogs to claw after governing power.

And they did not engage in long struggle and sacrifice just to throw open the floodgates for an endless stream of cronies, sycophants, job-seekers and other candidates whose main qualifications would consist of joining a party and "going along to get along".

Such things are all fruits of the party system.

The True Goal vs. Destruction

The development of *sound, independent judgment* among the people must be the goal of every true republican. Politicians who turn to elitism and manipulation become **destroyers** of a republic, worthy of the people's contempt.

The kind of "ideological aggression" discussed previously is rooted in a worldview wherein the people are seen as too stupid or venal to understand what is truly good for them. The superior group must therefore choose it on their behalf and impose it on them or simply manipulate them into it.

These are forces—i.e., ideological worldviews--most dangerous to a republic, which can be found hidden within political parties. Sadly, it seems inherent in the nature of our parties, in their 'DNA', to feature an elite group in their leaderships, an "inner ring."

The temptation to operate through manipulation of the public rather than through education and persuasion [education in the true sense of honestly presenting reality and history; not in the corrupt sense of "indoctrination"]; rather than by appealing to people's better judgment, will always be present.

RESTORE!

In restoring the original design of the Constitution, care must be taken toward making the approach of the Framers our own. This necessarily means re-discovering the motivating power and principles of the American Revolution.

Liberty is the chief among these principles and is the overarching context in which the Framers labored.

So one test of the result we seek should be that *political parties are at liberty to nominate whatever candidates they will. And the people also have the liberty (and the means) to nominate whatever candidates, drawn from private life, **they** will.*

It must always be clear that the parties have no "special right" to nominate. They do so ***only as citizens*** who have exactly the same right to nominate as all other citizens; and all other citizen groups (such as civic clubs, fraternal organizations, businessmen's groups, etc.). Parties have no more and no less right to nominate.

Consistent with this, a brief amendment might be adopted limiting information on the ballot to a candidate's name and place of residence; and forbidding mentions of race, religion, or affiliation (to a party, a union, a club or any other private organization).

There is no valid reason to allow the public ballot to be used for any private club or party's propaganda.

The club, or party, can pay for their own propaganda on billboards; or in other media if they want to establish the connection between them and their candidate.

Models of Government Contrasted

The great strength of a republic lies in its ability to seek out and choose from among the whole body of its people the most able, the most proven, the most honest, most talented and hopefully wisest of its citizens to lead the government. Whether this marvelous potential is actively being used or remains merely theoretical is a measure of the republic's health

An hereditary system of government rarely can accomplish this goal and therefore wastes the majority of a country's "talent pool" in favor of maintaining a certain class of persons—the hereditary elite.

The party system of government (parties only in control of government) also fails to accomplish this great goal and therefore also wastes the enormous reserves of a country's talent pool in favor of maintaining organized guilds of politicians and party workers.

The majority of these politicians and workers serve their party's clients, special interests, ideological camps--and themselves--while operating under the nominal banner of serving the country.

In the past there have been great Americans in each of the parties. There are also today a number of decent, capable people in government who, even though they are party members, belong where they are.

This is basically because the parties have been "the only game in town."

But the presence of this capable, decent minority who truly belong in government--either now or in the past--is not an accurate measure of how the parties really work. In fact, the "parties-only" system renders these people *unable* to provide the kind of honest government of which they are capable.

ELITES

Elites that seek to govern are by definition composed of strong, motivated personalities, no matter what their "area of focus" may be (military, religious, economic, or party-based). The human race will always contain some who are stronger, more organized, more cunning or persuasive, than others.

To stand out is one thing, usually the good result of a set of unique gifts.

But to predominate over others is entirely another matter. It is a motive not to be trusted and requires the most careful scrutiny because it so often involves hidden arrogance--a despising of those who are less brilliant, more "common".

What To Do With Them?

Constitutional government must be so designed as to afford opportunities for great service to highly gifted persons while at the same time putting up barriers against the possible formation of ruling elites who would usurp the functions of republican government

History shows that certain personalities tend to "rise to the top" no matter what form of government is in power. Capable, gifted persons are needed by parliaments, kings, and oligarchs alike to govern effectively.

The gifted strong personalities who tended to form elites have not disappeared from the earth. They are not automatically enemies of mankind. They are not the source of evil, as Jefferson assumed. They are simply gifted, but fallible, human beings.

The challenge to Constitutional government is to harness the great energy and capability of such persons in a way that *serves* the people, that provides them the opportunity to succeed and be recognized *in the service* of good government; but that does not permit subjugating others.

The Framers were well aware of the history of government by elites. To them, this was one of the chief dangers posed by political parties.

What has happened to America over the course of more than two centuries under the party system reflects this age-old struggle.

Our Constitutional system has done fairly well in stopping this human tendency (the taking of power by elites) but not well enough. In fact, party elites (not military or religious, etc.) have largely overcome this part of the Constitutional design.

The parties provide the most tempting entry point for elitist personalities who do not care for the people but see them as objects of manipulation to garner the maximum return possible for themselves and their allies.

The gathering of too much power into too few hands within the parties is simply a resurgence of this human failing, a surge by the strong toward governance by smaller (and therefore more elite) groups. This has been accomplished mostly within party ranks.

When combined with hubris, this party development (described in revealing detail, from an insider's perspective, by former Congressman Mickey Edwards in his book, "*The Parties Versus The People*") is leading our country toward deep, existential crisis.

How To Tell

A political leader who constantly seeks to strengthen himself and his party will prove in the end to have weakened and degraded his country.

The leader who consistently seeks to strengthen the *sound, independent judgment* (and freedom of action) of the people is the true republican.

Elitist personalities lean toward coercion to "get things done".

In fact, it is the coercive power inherent in government which often attracts these persons in the first place. They cannot really trust the people; but seek to manipulate or coerce them. Their twisted, immature values interpret such a pattern as "greatness". Such arrested-development personalities occasionally reach high office; but our media and universities are *overloaded*—packed to the rafters--with them.

The true leader is convinced that the only changes that are worthwhile are those which are freely chosen and agreed to in the hearts of the people. Such a leader will lead first by persuasion and example.

CHAPTER SEVENTEEN

Stable, Talented, And Responsive

Restoring the original design of the Constitution will also restore the Framers' vision for a stable, talented and responsive government.

Under the original design, the voters would have been able to do what a majority have nearly always wanted to do since then, but couldn't; which would be to take the best parts of each party's agenda and combine them into a stable ongoing plan of government.

Some of that did happen over the years through bipartisanship; but not nearly enough. The result has been "government by lurches" (from one party, to the other and back) -- the dysfunctional overall pattern of the party system, which has only gotten worse.

"Government by lurches" is a less-than-sane model. Long term, the people are frustrated and disgusted by this result of the party system. They need to know that this is not how representative government was meant to function; it is not what the Framers designed.

One outcome (when future voters are able to require the "merger" of their most favored parts of different party platforms into a stable ongoing plan of government) should be a government that rightly protects property and money but is not *obscenely dominated* by them as happens now through the parties.

When the Constitution is restored, the people will provide a counterbalance not only to the parties but also to the money which flows through the parties. As things are now, under party rule, there is an abuse and misuse of money which distorts our government into a corrupt form, not what it should be.

We must have a government which promotes sound independent judgment among the people as its permanent goal so that the people may forever refuse to be degraded by party leaders and ideologues into a *manipulocracy.*

CHAPTER EIGHTEEN

WHY "OF" + "BY" = "FOR"

When men make a plan based on their view of the world, then act upon that plan, they become invested in it. The more they act, the more invested they become.

Every degree of success they attain will tend to increase their sense of investment in the plan and its underlying philosophy. The result is that men will tend to repeat whatever course of action has led them to success.

This is a simple but deeply rooted trait in human nature: Men strongly tend to replicate those patterns that bring them success. This trait is obviously a rational one but its roots go deeper than reason. It is rooted in survival.

THE NEGATIVE SIDE

On the negative side, police investigations often depend on this trait. An "M.O.", or method of operation, is often the key to catching criminals who tend to repeat their more "successful" patterns of crime.

THE POSITIVE

On the positive side, the most successful businessmen are often those who have found a simple principle which works in their line of business, and have stuck with it. That principle may be as simple as using only fresh ingredients in a restaurant salad. But once good businessmen find a pattern that works they will stick with it because it brings success.

SAME TRAIT, BIGGER VENUE

This human trait also prevails in politics and government.

NEGATIVE

When fascist and Communist movements use assassination, intimidation, lies and bullets to gain power, only fools would imagine that they would somehow throw away their means of success once they seize that power.

Unfortunately they become locked into the use of coercion, fear, and force; into murder and intimidation to shape their societies. The resulting societies are abysmal human landfills full of abuse; of tyranny, fear and lying.

POSITIVE

On the positive side, this simple trait also predominates in honest business *and in honest politics.*

Political parties in early America rapidly took control of the new government simply by *organizing*. They made a ferociously concentrated (and coordinated) effort to win elections. This required increased levels of unified effort, money and agreed upon platforms, beyond anything seen before.

So...

The above information is 'background', leading up to the following:

American political parties, once they successfully attained power have followed the same human trait. They've stuck with what works, replicating their pattern of success.

Simply put, the national parties are at the same time:
    1.) interest groups.
    2.) umbrella organizations for other, smaller interest groups.

This may not seem like news at first. But it is: Those smaller interest groups are actually little parties. They are *organized and financed groups in pursuit of an agenda.*

The reality is that the big parties, having won power by being *organized and financed*, now govern primarily by attending to these "little parties" in pursuit of *their* well-financed, organized agendas.

The result is that ordinary citizens are really not the primary constituents of party government *unless and until they become organized into interest groups.*

At that point the big parties will take note and respond because they recognize that the money, effort, and votes which an *organized* little party (an interest group) can muster replicates their own success pattern. It therefore becomes "of consequence," and gets their attention.

It is for this reason that *when parties rule over the people* instead of the people ruling over parties, then lobbyists attain almost a semi-governmental role: They are spokesmen for the little parties which mirror the success pattern of the big parties and play by their rules.

So in a party system of government, interest groups (little parties) tend to form the main avenues of interaction and are the most important constituents of the big parties.

OF + BY = FOR

The result is no surprise. The primary focus of party government is: parties!

Ordinary, unorganized people are secondary. They are not completely unimportant; just very secondary. Until election time, when parties push out reams of rhetoric and promises.

Over time, the habit of governing through interest groups and lobbyists [which seems to save a lot of time] has produced a *political class* sorely out of touch with the people. Many of the people are deeply disillusioned, frustrated, and angry; but the political class (and their counterparts in the media) don't really understand why. They seem to think that everyone should be as happy with their performance as they are.

To sum up, a very strong tendency exists in politics and government. The means a group uses to gain power will usually become the means it uses to govern.

So, over time and in spite of their rhetoric, government *by* parties tends to become government *for* parties.

When *parties rule over the people,* instead of vice versa, the people are not the primary constituents of the government. Little parties are. The people become secondary, and they know it.

WHO RULES?

Government by parties inevitably leaves the common people with the sense that they are not really "in the loop" except as a sort of ratifier to be placated and manipulated every few years

Government "**of** the parties and **by** the parties" ends up being government "**for** the parties" (and for their clients and interest groups).

In the future, when the people rule over all parties (the Framers' design, restored) through **their own** elected representatives; when government "*of the people and by the people,*" at last returns to America, then we can expect that it will also be government "*for* the people."

In that future, parties and their clients will still be important; but they must be made secondary to the good, to the benefit, of the people.

CHAPTER NINETEEN

The Difference: Who is Judge?

To understand the difference between the Framers' design and what we endure today, we might picture a courtroom. The Framers' design has the people (through their elected representatives) as the Judge. The lawyers in this courtroom are the major parties (who act as spokesmen for clients and special interests).

The Framer's Design

Under the Framers' design, the Judge hears all sides of the argument and makes fair and honest rulings on each point in question.

VS. The Party System:

Under the party system the Judge does not occupy the bench but is seated to the side, with the spectators.

The two sets of lawyers now compete to see which will be "judge for a day".

When one side wins this competition and gets to sit on the bench, it starts issuing decision after decision in favor of its clients. When the opposing group of lawyers wins the bench they do likewise, changing previous rulings as often as possible.

The original Judge is reduced to sitting on the sidelines like a spectator. The only decision she's permitted to make is to designate, every two to four years, *which competing team of lawyers gets to take the bench* to make decisions and rulings in favor of themselves and their clients.

The result is slowly increasing chaos. There is growing tension and lack of civility *in* the court and drastically reduced respect *for* the court.

Some of the competing lawyers appear to be dignified. Others are arrogant or clownish. Some mock and insult their opponents. Others try to accommodate them, knowing that "their turn will come". But no matter how dignified the lawyers may try to look as they don judicial robes, under those robes they still have on their sharkskin suits. They are still lawyers--*partisan advocates for their clients*--and do not belong on the bench making rulings.

The bench, the place of judgments and rulings, belongs to the People.

HOW LONG?

How long will the American people put up with such distortion? There is a "double image" illustrated in the above story which corresponds to our party-dominated government. Partisan advocates put on robes and pretend to act as impartial judges, i.e., legislators.

In real life, our legislatures are filled by those who wear the robes of "representatives of the people" but who, underneath those robes, are partisans who chiefly represent *parties.*

Americans have been squinting at this double image for decades, trying to figure out "why things don't work".

"Is this how the Framers designed it?" we ask one another.

No!

is the answer of this book. What we have today–the party system-
-is *not* what the Framers designed.

It is time for Americans to say, "Enough!" of the degrading,
manipulative, and frequently vicious spirit of party.

THEY WERE RIGHT

After two centuries of experience we can say one thing with
certainty: The Framers were right about political parties and their
effects.

In spite of the Framers' marvelous design, parties have so damaged
the governance of the greatest Republic ever to exist that it has
become doubtful in the minds of many whether America *can*
recover.

CHAPTER TWENTY

The Constitutional Convention was composed of a number of the most capable, experienced and clear-minded political leaders of their time. They produced one of the most remarkable works in human history. In the opinion of some it is the greatest human document ever written.

The one thing they lacked, which no one on earth had at that time, was actual electoral experience in a large free republic. They could not foresee what two centuries of experience has revealed to us: *Checks and balances are as indispensable to the election process as they are within the actual structure of government.*

Experience has also revealed *that political parties are neither capable nor sufficient to fully check one another, that the only force capable of "checking and balancing" organized political parties is the sovereign power of the people themselves.*

This would form the ideal representative government. But for this ideal to be accomplished in practice, the people must be organized and given a format to work in by the Constitution itself through a Right to Nominate amendment. *Then* their sovereign power can be expressed, and the parties brought to heel.

The Right to Nominate is the key to America's recovery.

Providing a Mechanism

This Amendment—the Right to Nominate--will provide a mechanism for the American people to reach into their communities to find and nominate their own candidates for public office. Providing a real alternative, on every ballot, to any and all party candidates, is the appropriate course to pursue in correcting the one great weakness in the Framers' marvelous design.

This may be the only course capable of restoring the original design of the American Constitution. It is designed not only to restore a lost right, but to restore *lost liberty*—the liberty to vote for whom we truly *choose—and want to* vote for--instead of being forced to select from the restricted lists of defective party candidates constantly put before us.

For voters, this restricted choice is often like approaching a buffet of wilted and spoiled food, without anything else available to eat. This closed system, the party system, by limiting candidates to its own members, robs us of our liberty. The only question is: Why have we put up with this for so long?

200 Years of Experience, Applied:

Providing this Constitutional mechanism for the people to nominate their own candidates will accomplish a number of things:

1. The people will finally be able to search out and nominate persons whom they spontaneously respect and *want* to vote for due to their honest conduct and demonstrated abilities in non-political walks of life.

2. The people will be able to discipline and reject the lying and corruption that party politicians have steeped our elections in by voting **out** whatever proportion of all party politicians they choose, from both parties; and by replacing these politicians with whatever numbers they decide of representatives *drawn from the people*.

3. A balanced, non-lurching, and talented government can be obtained by the people also voting to retain whatever proportion

they decide of politicians from the parties who are, in their estimation, actually worthy of office.

The Likely Results

When a *checked and balanced* election system featuring both party and non-party candidates on every ballot reaches full operation, the proportion of party politicians found worthy to be retained in office will likely be sifted down to about 30%--roughly one out of three—of present office-holders.

A poll taken in October, 2013 by NBC/WSJ found that 60% of American voters favored a 100% turnover—a total replacement—of the members of Congress.

A Fox poll taken in March, 2014 found the proportion had risen to 67% in favor of total replacement.

But what good would total replacement of party politicians do, if they are simply replaced by more party politicians?

Voter Anger

Voters are deeply disillusioned and angry at the dysfunction of our present system.

Leaders in both parties are aware of this, but persist in seriously misinterpreting these results. One reason is that virtually all the polls have simultaneously found what a recent Gallup poll illustrates: there is a persistent, 20 point or more gap between how voters perceive "most" members of Congress, versus how they perceive "their" member.

So it is now common to hear pundits and party apologists comment on how, "Voters say they want to 'throw them all out'"; but then "turn right around and re-elect the same guys to office".

This condescending attitude comes from hubris and ignores the fact that most voters feel deeply responsible. They are generally unwilling to replace their representatives with unknown substitutes--not knowing what those "unknowns" will do--even though their anger and frustration level is real. (The polls are not wrong.)

So they reluctantly vote for a "known quantity". Not because they're happy to do it, but because their choices are so constricted. One party, or another (probably worse) party.

BUT WHAT WILL HAPPEN WHEN...?

What will the voters do when they are set free from the "prison shuffle" of party-run primaries and are able to vote for high-quality, known, well-vetted **non**-party candidates to represent them, drawn from their own communities?

Versus Party Cynicism

Another reason for the morbidity of this entrenched party attitude is a deeply-rooted cynicism, most often heard expressed after a primary election defeat by one wing of a party over another. In looking ahead to whether the losing wing will participate on behalf of the party in the general election, this cynicism is summed up as follows: "Where else can they go?"

In an overall sense, this cynical question also describes the hubris of party leaders, taken jointly (i.e., the party system) toward all unorganized voters.

Where Else Can They Go?
(THE ALL-IMPORTANT QUESTION)

With both parties thinking in these morbid terms [morbid-- accepting a disease that will prove fatal], and the media and academia as well, there is no locus of power now sufficient to check the degradation of American democracy by the party system.

Morbidity seems to be winning. And a third or fourth party would only make things worse; Americans have instinctively known this.

PROGNOSIS

The parties will not learn how wrong they are, how badly they've misread the voters, until Americans start nominating excellent candidates from their own communities and voting these into office; thus voting both parties *out*.

If the above proportion (about 30% of present officeholders, deemed worthy to stay in office) proves correct, then roughly two-thirds of party-affiliated officeholders will have to be replaced by persons who are genuinely the elected *representatives of the people,* selected by their own neighbors and peers to run for office; and then elected in fair and open competition against party nominees and self-nominated souls.

So, Is This "Power To The People"?

No.

That phrase, chanted in the streets in the 1960's, was drenched in hypocrisy and cynicism. It was a rallying cry for would-be revolutionaries. Its every utterance was fraudulent.

What lay behind it was the arrogant hypocrisy of Marxist ideology which states, "We (the Party and its leaders) are the only legitimate representatives of the people."

So who would actually get the power that was supposed to go "to the people"? The party leaders, of course. Only.

With what result? Dictatorship: tyranny and terror combined.

What a despicable, lying fraud that slogan was!

More than 150 million people were murdered in the 20th century by those who bought into that fraud; and by the intellectual fools who aided and abetted them.

Marxists do, however, exploit real needs in order to further their murderous, arrogant agenda.

So in a Far Different Sense,

Yes.

This book is aimed at restoring the rightful sovereignty of the people which was the basis of the Framers' original design.

Their design was a representative democracy, not direct democracy (a form that historically tended to degenerate into instability and demagoguery and to end up in tyranny).

Much of the rightful sovereignty of the people referenced by the Framers *has* been taken from the people. By whom? By none other than the parties and their leaders.

CHAPTER TWENY-ONE

Two centuries of experience have gradually revealed this missing right to nominate. When it is recovered, then true freedom of choice, *at the nomination stage,* bursting forth like abundant fruit on a newly matured tree, will finally come to our elections.

The crippling, dumb-'em-down effect on voters of being herded through a maze of pens and chutes, forced at each step to choose from a list of self-nominated or party-nominated candidates, can finally be scrapped. Nominating power will return to the whole community, as in the Framers' original design.

AFTER THAT

After that fundamental change, voters will always have a genuine choice: either vote for a party candidate; or vote for a non-party candidate nominated by a Jury/Convention.

The "parties-only" regime, with near-total control of the government perpetually held by party leaderships and handed back and forth between them must at last give way to the Framers' Constitutional design, wherein the people hold the overwhelming balance of power through *their* elected representatives.

All this must be accomplished in the context of liberty. This means perfect liberty for parties to nominate candidates; and now, *finally,* liberty for the people to nominate candidates too, which is their right.

Time and experience have at last yielded answers to us. We have caught sight of the best—and perhaps the only—way to restore the original design of the American Constitution.

Nominees for President

Nomination and election to the Presidency presented a special challenge, and received a whole separate treatment from the Framers: the Electoral College.

This seemingly makeshift system was actually highly rational. It was a parallel to the Framers' method for selecting U.S. Senators, and based on some of the same reasoning.

The College was intended to act as the final stage of a filtering process wherein men who had won great respect from their peers while working in the government over a long course of time could be nominated and elected.

Originally, each state legislature decided what the qualifications were for becoming an elector from that state. Each state got as many "electors" as they had delegates to Congress.

At first, many of the electors had the discretion to vote as they saw fit. But with the advent of fierce partisanship most states quickly bound their electors to vote according to the results of the popular ballot. The result was that "electors" began to function more as "transmitters" of the popular vote than as real electors of the President.

Nevertheless, it is still the votes of these electors in each state that legally elect a President and Vice President of the United States.

The Challenge, Updated

Nominating a candidate for President also presents challenges for Jury/Conventions. First, these bodies are designed to be nonpartisan. But when they begin their operations, most potential candidates for President with national experience and recognition will in reality be party politicians or individuals mostly identified with partisan causes.

It is imperative that the Jury/Conventions break out of the culture of the parties, out of partisanship, to set a new direction for America. This may prove more difficult than it first appears.

If the Jury/Conventions were allowed to nominate prominent members of either party for President, for example, then the full spin and strife of partisan campaigning would come to bear on them, both from party candidates and from the media.

It would be difficult for the Jury members to keep their heads on straight, let alone set a new direction to change American political culture.

But since the Jury/Conventions will be barred by law from nominating party members, there will be a lull, a hiatus, for a time. This will last until enough non-partisan candidates have been elected to legislative and judicial offices and have had sufficient time in those offices to build up a record.

By then there will likely have emerged men and women who would make excellent candidates for President who have built a national reputation for honesty, competence and vision.

So the Jury/Conventions should not nominate candidates for the Presidency during the first twelve to fifteen years of their inception. Each state should then decide when to begin considering nominations for President.

CHAPTER TWENTY-TWO

The Coming Contest

Our political parties have in their ranks a few of the most amoral, nastiest and toughest people on earth. At the same time, they have some of the most persuasive, "golden tongued" talkers on earth. And it is not so uncommon to find that these traits can reside in the same individuals.

The parties are not going to give up their stranglehold easily. Taken together, they have complete control over our governments. Together, they have taxed, borrowed and spent **TRILLIONS** more dollars than the people have in the Treasury.

How Much?

Try this: Google "How much is a trillion dollars?" Find your favorite illustration; there are a number of good ones.

One illustration asks, "If you were offered a billion seconds to live, how long would that be?" Answer: about 32 more years.

That sounds reasonable, or at least understandable.

"So how long would a *trillion* seconds last you?" Answer: you'd have about 32,000 more years to live.

That sounds ludicrous, incomprehensible.

This unimaginably huge national debt (19 TRILLION dollars as of early 2016) has been abusive of the people's trust on an epochal scale.

Hubris

James Madison referred to arrogance in *Federalist # 37 as* one of the "infirmities and depravities of the human character." It is the destructive, prideful response of human nature to great success.

"Hubris" is the ancient name for it.

Success plus a lack of competition, are the only conditions required for this kind of arrogance, or hubris, to hold sway.

Instances abound in history. General Motors and the rest of our automobile industry had established such overwhelming success by the 1960's that they seemed untouchable, on top of the world.

Hubris set in, to the extent that these manufacturers began to design and sell "planned obsolescence," i.e., vehicles that were designed to break down after a certain amount of time, forcing the customer to buy a new one.

This fat-headed arrogance was only curtailed when foreign competition, notably from Japan, began to rip huge chunks of market share away from Detroit simply by building better cars. It took decades for American car makers to begin to catch up.

The American steel industry followed a similar path: hubris followed world domination; which then resulted in decline on the heels of severe foreign competition.

America's labor movement evidenced a similar arc. First there was a righteous cause, then hard-won success. This led to a sense that success and power were locked in. But hubris entered, then abuses, and finally decline.

Same Pattern:

Our two major parties have followed this same human arc
from "striving" to "success," and from success to hubris. They
are presently at the top of their arc, seemingly untouchable.
Nonetheless they are sowing the seeds of their own destruction and
the destruction of our Republic through arrogant acts.

They tie our government down, paralyzing it through the mindless
ill will of partisanship. The people feel helpless to stop them. They
ruinously, irresponsibly, run up enormous national debt. They go
on in patterns they know American voters hate. Why?

Well, why not?

Because taken *together* as a system, the parties are "locked in" to
power, untouchable.

Their long successful record ("successful" in the sense that *together,*
as a system, they've held onto power and seemed unchallengeable,
'forever'). But their long history of control over the government
has at last overbalanced the sense of caution they once maintained
because of ever-upcoming elections.

Control of the legislative branch may shift back and forth in those
elections. They do worry about that. But that has happened many
times. They've learned it will not affect their tandem, seemingly
permanent, control of the government. That is the real source of
their hubris, especially in the leaderships.

The hubris of entrenched power long ago set in. The parties, taken
together, have reason to think they are "locked in," producing a
corporate attitude like General Motors and U.S. Steel had in the
1960's.

The arrogance of this party hubris has shown itself recently in potentially catastrophic, irresponsible budgetary actions and in gridlock. In these crises the parties have shown little or no concern for competently serving the people or for being accountable to them.

The people must understand that the essential condition for this hubris to be "locked in" to the parties is that:

THEY HAVE NO REAL COMPETITION.

General Motors only turned around when Japanese automakers started squeezing the fat out of their heads, the fat of complacency that comes with hubris. By the time they finally "got lean" and competitive they had lost an enormous chunk of their market share.

"Competition" from other American automakers didn't accomplish this result; they were far too similar to GM in their thinking. It took **REAL COMPETITION.**

Hubris produces ghastly, insane results in every field of human endeavor; from movie-making to manufacturing to military strategy; but especially in governance.

If "We, the people" do not stand up and re-establish the Framers' design for our Constitution and bring **REAL COMPETITION** to all parties, by redeeming our Right to Nominate, we could lose our country and lose it soon.

Ahead

Though the parties have their histories which include much to answer for, such as slander, greed, manipulation, voter fraud, etc., they each also include a minority of decent, honorable people who truly belong in government. These members would be willing to provide honest government if they could.

But the soft coercion (and the hidden iron hand) of the party system makes that impossible.

The phrase, "honest members" refers to those members who have a degree of integrity, whose "word is good," who don't take one position in public but another behind closed doors, who don't award their friends contracts and jobs, who don't lie constantly or drain the public treasury to enhance their own careers, who don't tailor their oversight of regulatory panels with an eye for the "revolving door" of a lobbyist's job later on, and similar commonsense criteria.

How many such people are there?

It would be impossible to get a "scientifically accurate" answer to this question.

Each one attempting to answer it would begin from a unique set of opinions and values. For anyone answering, there would be a tendency to rate their friends and allies highly; and their opponents as much worse.

So, subjective answers are the best we can get by asking officeholders to evaluate other officeholders. The most important thing to consider before asking for such an evaluation is, "How much do I trust the thinking and values of the person I'm asking?"

When posed with this question, "In light of your experience, what proportion of present officeholders would you *turn the government over to,* based on their honesty, ability and integrity, *regardless of party*, and expect them to govern well?"

Answers have ranged from 25 percent (from the ranks of conservative, experienced legislators) to anywhere on a scale of 0 to 82 percent (from the non-office-holding public, according to polls).

Despite the difficulties involved, such questions must be asked. Voters need to know how other officeholders rate their own representative's integrity and honesty. No voter would be happy to learn that many members of Congress consider their representative to be ineffectual, two-faced, a "go along" hack, a crook, or a hypocrite.

But if our estimate is true (that about 30 percent—one out of three-- of present officeholders would give us honest government if put in charge), then it's also true that this honest minority must now constantly contend with the roughly *65 to 70 percent majority* who belong to the party system as it is and have given us what we now have.

If this were not so, we would not have ended up where we are now.

This minority (it exists in both parties) can't yet do what it would do: provide honest government. However, the public should be aware that this minority exists; it is not inconsequential.

When push comes to shove and votes are taken on an Amendment to protect and to provide for the Right to Nominate, we will all be relying on these honest members of the government to stand up for us and to *stand* for our rights.

2 OUT OF 3 MUST GO

However long it takes to win back the people's Right to Nominate, it will certainly involve election after election in which the voters sift all officeholders, *getting rid* of those who deny their rights or act behind closed doors to hinder them.

By consistently voting out of office every politician opposing the people's Right to nominate, American voters will decide whether or not the Constitution will be restored to its original design. They will decide whether to end automatic party control of government; or not.

At the same time voters must be aware of who their friends are. These are the ones from either party who support their Right to Nominate, in public and in private. Voters must consistently reward them.

The Goal, And The Aim

The goal is to restore the Right to Nominate to voting Americans through amendment and to pass all legislation necessary to provide for exercising this right.

So America now stands at the brink of a momentous change toward greater freedom and restored power for her citizens. How we bring that change about will determine what kind of life we will have once the change is made.

Restoring the lost Right to Nominate will permanently enhance the power of each American vote. The rightful sovereignty lost to the parties will be taken back vote by vote, in election after election, by Americans who genuinely and fiercely treasure "*..government of the people, by the people, and for the people.*"

But this increasing power in the voters' hands ought to be used in the most practical way possible, even while the lost Right is being re-won.

Voters' aims during this time should be two-fold:

1.) To promote those who support the people's rights, getting rid of those who don't.

2.) To identify the decent one-third of current officeholders who comprise the honest minority and then vote consistently in such a way as to turn the government over to them, in concert with newly elected citizen Nominees.

This will obviously present a challenge because virtually all office-holding politicians are likely to claim that they've *always* been part of the honest minority! How are voters to know who is lying?

CHAPTER TWENTY-THREE

A Better Boss

If America's government and political culture are to fully mature, if corruption is to be reduced to a minimum and an ongoing Civil Discourse established, then the most essential change is this: We the people must become a better boss.

Americans have become cynical and make a lot of jokes about politicians. We talk like they are some alien race of reptiles who periodically land in a field, put on plastic masks to look human, and then wriggle off to hire campaign managers.

We don't like to look at our part in all this. A big part of the reason politicians dissemble and say so little is that we often will cut them down and crush them if they say something honest *that we don't like*. (While the parties just keep on going.)

A good boss wouldn't act like that.

The more power we accumulate in our votes, then the more we can enforce some dignity from political candidates, by getting rid of slanderous and negative campaigners; and by working steadily through our votes to establish a Civil Discourse.

We have to change our political culture. One place to start is to reward honesty with respect even if it comes from a viewpoint we disagree with.

Using Landmarks

Earned respect as the right road to advancement would represent a fundamental change in our political culture. It contains promise for a positive effect on the general culture as well; because it would consistently acknowledge and reward lives lived well.

As things are now, our media tend to emphasize and celebrate all kinds of bizarre, irresponsible behavior with a sort of sophomoric glee, often conveying the impression of a culture unraveling.

A Good Decision

Adopting a system of public nomination through Constitutional amendment will entail a commitment to acknowledging (and in a sense, rewarding) lives well-lived, giving our young people an incentive to aim at making better life choices.

This is likely to generate an ongoing discussion about what it means to live life well, which would be a healthy thing in itself for a republic. It would provide a healthy counterpoint to the degrading and pointless *lack* of value found in our entertainment and news media.

Pop culture's portrayal of our politics is usually dark; filled with deceit, cynicism, hypocrisy and manipulation of the public. (Usually unspoken and unexamined is the fact that the creators of such portrayals are often at least as full of negative traits as the characters they portray.) But, sadly, these depictions are not all wrong; and they are constantly being displayed before our youth.

We need to change our political culture: the cynical, manipulative, lying *party* culture; so that our youth have something more noble to aim at.

BACK TO THE JURY/CONVENTIONS:
FIRST, ISSUE A COMMENTARY

Consistent with its overall purpose the first action of a Jury/ Convention should be to take a day or two to put together a Commentary, or Report, on the last campaign, on its candidates and its results. In particular, the Report should evaluate how well the words and promises of the winning candidate (whether party or non-party) were later *matched* by their performance in office.

If the candidate promised much and delivered little, this would be noted in the Jury/Convention's Commentary. If he or she polluted the campaign with negativity or slander, this also would be noted. If the candidates used fear-mongering, or said anything they knew at the time to be untrue this would be prominently stated.

THEN, EVALUATE THE MEDIA

This commentary should also evaluate the role of media and news outlets during the same period.

Americans will not tolerate any loss of freedom for the press. But we are also frequently disgusted in seeing the abuse of that freedom *by* the press; and it would be a healthy thing for the people to have their voice finally heard, to evaluate the press' performance. And how they believe that performance (or lack thereof) has affected our public life.

From a Prepared List

For the sake of efficiency, a list of predetermined questions should be used to form the foundation of this Commentary, questions included as part of the <u>instructions to the Jury.</u> The yeas and nays of the Jury are recorded for each question; with the purpose of *holding candidates accountable* for what they say during campaigns, and do later when in office

With the combination of these Jury Reports (which would give the people an official voice, a way to publicly evaluate the performance of politicians) and the example set through respectful dialogue during Jury interviews of prospective Nominees (i.e., through Civil Discourse) we will take giant steps toward making "We, the people" a better, more 'hands-on' boss.

This is the objective: to develop *sound judgment in the people* and to restore a sense of ownership and responsibility to a large part of our citizenry.

It may take a generation or more to reverse the effects of *manipulocracy,* that destroyer of republican mentality by which the party system has degraded our Republic.

Sound judgment among the people must be the goal of every true republican.

But in direct contrast, the effects of a two-party manipulocracy on our people presently include cynicism, hopelessness and irresponsibility becoming so widespread that they seem normal.

"...if you can keep it."

When the Federal Convention wrapped up its work in September of 1787 and the delegates emerged from their last meeting a woman in the crowd outside the hall asked Benjamin Franklin, "Sir, what kind of government have you given us?"

"A republic, madam, if you can keep it," was Franklin's timeless, sobering reply.

CHAPTER TWENTY-FOUR

But

The movement to redeem the people's Right to Nominate will appear to some elements within the parties as a thing to be warred against. These amoral individuals will not interpret the issue as one of American freedom versus the suffocating party control of government.

It will simply be seen as a threat to their hidden lock on power and perks.

The secret to their dual lock on power has flown beneath the public's radar for many years. Their secret is to control access to the ballot, as Congressman Mickey Edwards has ably described.

"Gerr"-ked Around

Gerrymandering is an exercise in arrogance. Both parties do it. By redrawing district boundaries, the parties can basically *neutralize* tens of thousands of votes. Spread over hundreds of districts, this number reaches into the millions of votes. If you live in a "gerried" district, your vote may already have lost much of its power. Many commentators use the word *"disenfranchise"* to describe this effect.

But if your vote could talk, the word *"disembowel"* would communicate the effect better.

Reduced to its essence, gerrymandering is about increasing the power of the parties by decreasing the power of the voters. When the parties do this kind of exercise they reveal their true underlying character.

What those who engineer gerrymandering care about is their own party's status and power and the perks that come with that. What they could care less about is the bedrock American value of fairness.

Bring *that* value up in a meeting of party honchos redrawing district lines and you'd likely see reactions ranging from stony stares to rolled eyes. Sound effects might range from snorts to chuckles.

But that reaction would not last long. Our parties have become so adept at spin that, as soon as their surprise wore off, these party honchos would have their best speaker reassuring you that,

"No, no, no; we're *working hard* here to **maintain** fairness! Because if we don't do this to them, they'll for sure do it to us. And then things will get all out of balance!"

There are decent people in both parties, but they are *not in charge*. The vile, arrogant practice of gerrymandering reveals who is in charge.

"…it will rarely happen.."

"It will rarely happen that the advancement of the public service will be the primary object either of party victories or of party negotiations."
Federalist #76(5)

"Ringer" Candidates

There are many ways the parties control access. One way is to put up "ringer" candidates when the leadership wants to 'take down' an officeholder who's gotten non-compliant. A few years ago, a Hispanic lady in the Illinois legislature became so well-liked and respected that her Democratic colleagues spontaneously elected her leader of their caucus.

Bad mistake: They hadn't gotten permission from the party bosses. In the next election cycle a few months later the bosses put up another Hispanic candidate in her party's primary to run against her. The Hispanic vote was split; the lady lost her office.

Party leaders in general are realists, not racists. But they know perfectly well how to take advantage of ethnic voting blocks.

The party bosses were relieved of the nuisance of having someone around who hadn't sufficiently knuckled under. One less representative from their party made no difference to them.

But the classic use of a "ringer" candidate, in a gambit used countless times, is to put up a little-known name to run a hopeless primary race against a known but boring party favorite.

The party favorite already has the nomination sewed up; the ringer's job is furnish the illusion of a horse race; a 'PR' stunt to boost public interest and to avoid the "wilted and stale" label that the party's candidate probably deserves.

Such ringers are put forward to lose; in return, they are rewarded with well-paying government jobs.

Americans would do well to consider the learning curve that our early diplomats and Presidents had to go through concerning foreign relations. It took time for some of them to learn that nation-states don't have friends, they have interests. (Interestingly, George Washington knew this from the beginning; he needed no learning curve.)

George Washington's Example

In a similar vein many American voters today would be better off if they adopted the stance that political parties don't have friends, but only interests. This will require discarding illusions produced by the political tradition of 'glad-handing' (of pretending sympathy for anyone with a complaint or a cause).

American politicians generally must meet the minimum requirement of having some people-skills in that they must be able to act friendly. This hardly means they are your friends.

A friend doesn't smile and greet you warmly one day and then go to a meeting the next where your district is *gerrymandered* and your vote is eviscerated and you are left without being told by your party friend that it happened. News accounts of this kind of *party fraud* tend to be vapid or use terms like "shenanigans," as if the readers are supposed to chuckle.

The cumulative effect of the various devices parties use to control access to the ballot have left a large number of voters with the uneasy sense that we, as a people, have lost control of our government; that it is now owned by parties, by politicians and by special interests. There are some who no longer vote because they perceive it as a wasted effort.

Voter Power

America's Founding generation was the first in history to not only *found* a Republic but to carefully deliberate, to decide how self-government in that republic should be designed.

Now, after two centuries we find the design corrupted, with much of our *self-government* subtly altered to government *by parties.*.

The Right to Nominate the key to restoring the Framers' original design. But it is also the missing cornerstone of representative democracy itself, which means that more than the fate of America is at stake.

The Right to Nominate is crucial to any people's ability to "keep" a republic, in the sense of Ben Franklin's admonition. In our case, without this Right being protected and *used,* power has steadily leaked from the people's hands into the hands of those who seek the power for themselves and their cronies.

Its omission from the Bill of Rights has allowed government by elite groups (in our case, *party elites*) to creep in, grow like a tumor and displace our original form of government.

That original form, designed as a true republic, was described by Abraham Lincoln as "government of the people, by the people, and for the people." He called it…*"the last, best hope of mankind."*

THE LAST, BEST HOPE

When men fail to be civilized, warlords rule them. If men cannot operate together with agreed-upon principles and rules, then brute force wielded by thugs must eventually organize them. Warlordism is humanity's default form of government.

It is also the lowest and worst form of society, with little respect for life, liberty or human rights.

What Abraham Lincoln referred to was the history of human government, which has most often seen men governed (or misgoverned) by elites. The focus of these elites has varied but the fact has not. Military power has been the most frequent type of elite rule. But elite rule focused around religion, great wealth, hereditary status or ideology have all been common in history.

Each form of elite rule has historically proven unreliable, in terms of fair and honest government. Misrule and abuse of the people has been the tragic end result, in varying degrees, for each of them.

In blunt terms, history demonstrates that the common people had better have sufficient power in their hands to watch out for themselves or else *some* elite group will find a way to abuse them.

But history also shows that "pure" democracy, with the people controlling all power directly, does not work. The people themselves get "out of control" and commit abuses.

Representative democracy has given us the best solution in recorded history for this problem.

But restricting freedom of choice to only two groups [i.e., parties] from which to choose candidates essentially destroys the advantages of representative democracy. This party-benefitting restriction on our freedom of choice insures that thousands upon tens of thousands of capable, respected independent figures are never even *considered* for public office. They are simply left out by the party system; their talents are wasted.

A party system in any country trends toward the formation of party elites; and this, in turn, leads into domination of the electoral system by money. Only Constitutional nominations can break the fierce and intractable hold of money over the Nomination stage of our elections.

The Big Detour

Our Republic took a detour when the party system took over, a detour that has ended up in dysfunction and political degradation; and in the ominously literal looming bankruptcy of our country.

Detours are temporary. It is time to get back to the main highway and build a genuine republic.

Thankfully, our roots are **NOT** in the party system. They are in the Constitution and in the Framers, whose marvelous work—the American Constitution--was birthed from an anti-party worldview.

The Nasty Surprise

Historian Ron Chernow has recently shown how George Washington was taken by surprise--astonished at how fast the venom of party slanders and partisan undermining began to move into the new Republic during the mid-to-late 1790's.

So were John Adams, John Marshall and many other good men.

As blighting as the effects of party have been, they can never detract from the greatness of what the Founders accomplished. They did perhaps the greatest work in the history of human government by writing and adopting the Constitution.

But those who later brought in party-ism, the partisan mentality, defiled our Constitution, our history, and their own names forever.

Party tactics in our country were born in divisiveness and egoism; and nursed on deception, malice and slander.

Debating wise policy choices was not how the party system won out. It won through slander and character assassination; through undermining opponents by malicious accusation and innuendo. That pattern continues to this day, in party campaigns.

"That pattern continues to this day."

Slander is <u>not</u> the necessary part of civil debate that party apologists and incompetent op-ed writers would have us believe.

In fact, slander ruins civil debate. It poisons and destroys Civil Discourse.

Slander, and malicious lying, will poison civil discourse in <u>any</u> human community. Slander, to use an accurate, ancient description many now avoid, is *evil*.

Is Anything Good About Parties?

Without irony or sarcasm this is what's good about parties: they have some decent people in them. Unfortunately, these people do not predominate.

The very best thing about parties is that they have an abundance of human relationships both within themselves and outwardly. When relationships are good, or even just decent, then politics can be healthy.

Conversely, every **detestable** product of party politics ultimately boils down to violations committed in human relationships, in how people are viewed or treated.

Consider the list of party wrongs: slander, enmity, lying, manipulation, fraud, corruption, insider deals, hypocrisy, hubris and so on. They are all violations of human relationship, either at a personal or criminal level.

The Great Promise

The great promise in all this is that the people, when they regain their missing Right and thus have genuine choices, are more than able to discipline the parties and party politicians out of lying, exaggerating, waste, manipulation, slander and the whole panoply of party wrongs. The people are more than able to recognize these violations. They just need a viable **non**-party alternative in order to be able to enforce their moral will. But short of encountering this kind of voter force, the parties cannot and will not change.

Enter, A Better Boss

The people must regain their rightful sovereignty so that by the power of their votes (those cast for non-party candidates), they can *force* the parties to either change their ways; become transparent and *serve* the people (instead of fleecing them); or be pushed aside, off the center stage of American history.

REORGANIZE CONGRESS

The organization of Congress was mostly left to the integrity of those elected by the people in the Framers' original plan. It should have worked; but when parties took over the government, the built-in dysfunction of the party system invaded Congress. Another of the Framers' great designs was badly damaged.

The trust inherent in the Framers' design has been abused by the parties, giving us today's dysfunctional Congress. We now have inherited the task of re-organizing Congress into what it should always have been: the place where the people's business is done; and not an arena for party posturing and jousting.

Nothing can stop individual legislators from posturing and jousting. But Congress can and should be re-organized into a non-partisan form in its committees and voting procedures through Constitutional Amendment.

The people's votes must discipline the parties out of their "wheel & deal" egotism culture into a more competent and responsible mindset of service. This will be such an enormous change that it can only happen over a period of time. It *requires* redeeming the people's Right to nominate.

As was the case with General Motors it can only happen through **real competition** being brought to bear on the parties, in the context of liberty. This competition must be able and willing to push the parties aside, into vestigial status.

If the parties cooperate they won't become a vestige. But if they fight against the people's Right to Nominate they will make themselves *illegitimate* and will have to be pushed aside, off the center stage of American history.

So the people must be ready for this. They must be ready for a long campaign, possibly over a generation or more.

But if the people are willing and stay with the task the world may one day witness a 'new thing', another "**first**" coming out of America: a renewed, genuine Republic, no longer in partisan decline, restored and matured, filled with Civil Discourse; *where political parties have been brought to heel,* brought into serving the people; not lying to, fleecing or manipulating them.

Does this sound like a dream? Good: because America is where things that may have seemed like *impossible dreams* in other cultures, or in other times, get done.

But they don't get done by merely dreaming. They take work. Americans are practical. This dream is do-able, but only through the **application of power**—the restored sovereign power of the people's votes--over time.

CHAPTER TWENTY-FIVE

Summing Up

We have now examined our own history with the same uniquely American sense of purpose that the Framers used in examining history prior to themselves: to find out what has worked in the past; what has not; and why.

We've seen that the Framers carefully crafted a system of checks and balances for the new government of America which were intended to *limit the effects* of party.

We've examined those planned checks in detail and seen how quickly most of them were overwhelmed by the ferocious advent of *organized,* major parties.

Our examination of this history has led to an unavoidable conclusion: The magnificent design of the Constitution, as brilliant as it was, could not work as the Framers intended because of one flaw: all the careful checks and balances it featured were embodied *within* the structure of the new government.

But the political parties based their pursuit of power *outside* the structure of government: by organizing to win elections.

We've determined that Constitutional *checks and balances* are as necessary in elections as in the structure of government; or else organized parties will overwhelm those elections. They will take control of the government away from the people, and thus take away the peoples' sovereignty.

Finally: we've found through long, difficult experience that the party system is ruinous; it does not work.

The goal of this book is to walk in the steps of the Framers, to "take men as we find them," and to carefully implement an added Constitutional structure which can handle men *as we've found them* over the course of more than two hundred years.

This book promotes a system embodied in an Amendment that can *handle* party tendencies toward greed, aggression and secretiveness--which will keep cropping up again and again, no matter what reforms may temporarily be in effect.

Our goal is to restore the original design of the American Constitution by bringing its brilliant *checks and balances* design into our election system, thereby restoring the people's sovereignty.

Our goal necessarily includes breaking the stranglehold of the "parties-only" system and restoring the original vision of the Framers for a "mixed" government in which the people have the *upper hand* over all parties through their elected representatives. This was the Framers' intention and design.

We intend to restore the upper hand embedded in the Framers' design by restoring to the people their lost Right to Nominate; (specifically, to nominate **non**-party candidates).

Then, in the context of liberty, let the people always make the final choices.

In Conclusion:
THE PERFECT PICTURE

...showing where we are; and what work lies ahead, comes from Nature and the terrible results of human abuse:

When Europeans first landed in North America, they found a huge unspoiled continent with an astonishing abundance of animal and plant life. There were forests full of old-growth timber, great herds of animals, flocks of birds, rich soil and great clean waterways. It was far and away the best land discovery since prehistoric times.

Then, in Abraham Lincoln's words, our forefathers "*...brought forth on this continent a new nation, conceived in liberty...*"

In 1788, barely over two hundred years ago, both the huge continent filled with natural beauty and abundance; and the new nation filled with hope, and with the glory of freedom, seemed poised for a great, unstoppable destiny.

Natural beauty and human achievement both abounded in this new nation.

But before long, destructive things began to be done in both the natural and the political realms. And there was an unnoted, remarkable parallel between them.

In the natural realm we cut down whole forests, nearly exterminated the bison, fished out many lakes and rivers, killed a huge proportion of the wildlife, polluted rivers and lakes with toxic waste and nearly lost our heritage of rich soil through erosion. We strip-mined and clear-cut and polluted our way almost to the point of devastation. And we did all that in less than 180 years.

Thank God, we've been able to stop much of that destruction. And we've begun to turn some of it around. Our rivers and lakes are much cleaner now. Toxic dump sites are rarer. Our wildlife is better managed.

Best of all, our national mentality has changed to a great degree. We are much more aware of the treasures we have in Nature and of our duty to preserve them into the future.

But doesn't this leave an unanswered question: What are we to think of previous generations? They were our ancestors.

Should we revile their memory because they left environmental damage? Are we somehow superior to them?

Not at all. The prevailing thought patterns during much of that history included creating homes out of wilderness lands, feeding and providing for families and wading into an incredible opportunity for creating prosperity and riches from what looked like an inexhaustible supply of resources.

They saw themselves as creating and building communities and bringing civilization into an almost empty, sometimes savage, land. They were well aware of the dangers, the challenges and the backbreaking work that would be involved. The history of our pioneers is one of the greatest stories in the saga of human endeavor, a tremendous story of courage and hard work.

And Yet,

And yet, we almost destroyed the ecosystem of an entire magnificent Continent. We almost ruined the greatest natural Gift that any people group has ever received--the gift of an unspoiled, beautiful, magnificent, virgin Continent.

There is more than a lesson here. "Lesson" is far too small a word. There is a *revelation* in this story that speaks to every age of human existence.

One part of the revelation (which may sound insignificant, but most certainly is not) is this: Whatever we as humans may *think* we're doing, ("we" being any people group or culture in its time of greatest vigor); it is almost certain to turn out to be "not the whole story." (Including our generation's positive mandate to restore the environment.)

Humility is an eternal virtue. It should always be paired with strength. It can keep individuals and nations from committing terrible mistakes. Adhering to eternal values is the best way to go through life successfully, for nations as well as individuals.

Our ancestors, the pioneers, were *not* all wrong. Most of what they thought had good intent. Most of it was right. Much was tremendously admirable.

But they did not deal rightly with Nature, so we--their descendants--inherited a duty to make up for that, to set right a massive amount of harm done to the natural environment.

THE PARALLEL

During the same time that destructive practices were ruining our natural environment, *parallel destructive practices* wreaked by the parties were ruining our political environment, polluting and poisoning American minds.

The parallel is astonishing; and it is far more than coincidence.

The rip-off and rape of the natural realm, the abrasive lack of care or stewardship, the "fast buck" abuses of Nature were being *perfectly matched* by the rip-off and rape of American culture: the slanderous, community-destroying abuse done by ideologues and partisans.

The soul of the American people was being battered and exploited. Externally free, yes; but the minds of newly self-governing Americans were being *toxic-dumped*, strip-mined and left gaping at the sky, as it were, by the slander, lies, and corrupt manipulations of partisan politics.

Honor?
Community?
Truth?

Who cares? if the object is to win at all costs. And if the fastest way to win–the "fast buck" of politics–is to shove your opponent's name and reputation into a sewer?

Shove him in! Dunk him, before he dunks you!
"Politics ain't beanbag", right?

Right.

Politics, under the party system 'ain't' a lot of things. It ain't clean. It ain't honest. It ain't competent to solve our problems *or* produce good government. It ain't something that our more honest citizens would want to be a part of.

We'd better change that before we lose our Republic.

What we've experienced politics to be, *under the party system,* is exactly what the Framers said they would be if parties were involved: **"poisoned"**, **"tainted"**, **"infected"**, **"diseased"**, **"perverted"**, **"intolerant"**, **"malignant"**, and **"foul-breathed"**. (Every one of these words comes straight out of the *Federalist Papers.)* **"Party rage"**, these Founding authors said, would break out; and the power of appointment would be **"prostituted"**.

The days of chuckling at party abuses and putting up with waste and destruction are finished. It is time for Americans to say, "**To hell** with the **spirit of party**!" before we lose our Republic.

The verdict is in: the Framers were right. Their warnings are as fresh and powerful and accurate now as in the days they were first penned.

Equal Blight, Plus Some

We are living today in a blighted and polluted *political* landscape that more than matches the blight and pollution of our natural environment at its worst point.

The bright hope generated by a true Republic, which came into this world with the birth of America and uplifted all humanity, has been soiled by the toxic dumpsites and poisoned waters of party politics.

Toxic mental dumpsites created by the parties now lurk in American minds and continually leak their poison into our discourse and into our thinking.

They *have to* be cleaned up.

In contrast to the natural environment, this cleanup has not yet begun. It can't until the people redeem their Right to Nominate.

RESTORE

As with the natural environment, we have inherited a duty to clean up the toxic waste the parties have dumped into our politics and into our culture; and to restore the clean air and water of Civil Discourse that should be the inheritance of all who are born into a republic.

It is our responsibility to restore the original design of the American Constitution and thus end *unchecked party control* of our government.

In the context of Liberty, one shining, hopeful principle provides the foundation for accomplishing this goal:

The Right to Nominate belongs to the people.

Epilogue

The End of An Age

We Americans initiated the most recent epoch of man's history, often called the Age of Revolution. In the two hundred thirty-odd years since our revolution the world has seen numerous upheavals and overthrows, most of them violent. In the twentieth century alone, more than 140 million people died, directly or indirectly, as a result of violent revolutions.

The idea of revolution itself was perverted during this time by ideologues into a systematic conquest of existing governments, some oppressive, others not.

In most cases the governments resulting from these imposed revolutions, initiated by ideologues and carried out by professional revolutionaries were more thuggish, tyrannical and oppressive than anything seen before, following the dictum that the means a group uses to gain power will also be the means they use to rule.

Revolution itself was perverted from its most pure form, a spontaneous assertion of human rights and liberties. It was perverted by party ideologues into a mask for aggression using assassination, propaganda and guerilla war as means to power.

The concept of revolution itself was hijacked to serve as cover for ideological wars of conquest.

This tragic and bloody history, like all human conflict, has been played out against a backdrop of invisible but determinative moral values.

Who is right? Does a corrupt or oppressive government justify violent revolution? How corrupt or oppressive does it have to be?

Should the 200-plus existing governments in the world be viewed as competitors in a Darwinian marketplace in which the most stupid and corrupt ones become fair game for revolutionaries? Or for religious fanatics murdering and conquering in the name of God?

Is it right for revolutionaries to become aggressors, bullying and intimidating rural populations, assassinating local leaders, press-ganging youth into a guerilla army and "taxing" the local population, as is done by Marxist revolutionaries? Is all of this justified by claims to a moral right based on opposition to "oppressive government"?

What about that local population caught between the brutality against them by a regime run by economic or military elites versus the brutality against them by revolutionary aggressors waging guerilla war, abetted by intellectual elites in distant countries? (Elites who have exposed their intellectual and moral bankruptcy by choosing to adopt the insane position that it is possible to murder, confiscate, lie and coerce one's way to a just society?)

Our sympathies should lie with these brutalized people, treated like pawns, caught between two powerful warring factions (the old elite regime versus the new, aggressive ideological one), both of which claim the right to decide their fate for them.

Universal Right

It seems self-evident that the universal spread of the Right to Nominate will put an end to elite oppressive regimes, whether of the old model or the newer ideological one.

It will put an end to this terrible Age because:

Normal people are aware of where their interests lie. They are even more aware of who has done evil to them; or who has treated them well. No people group is so blind or oblivious to its own interests that it would *freely* nominate men who are known to be cruel, perverted or unjust to govern them.

So the spread of this universal Right can put an end to most of the *need* for revolution.

It can surely put an end to the kind of "revolution" which treats unorganized populations as designated prey for ideological aggressors fighting wars of conquest under a nominal banner of revolution.

Time To End It

We Americans kicked off this Age of Revolution.

It is now up to us, by redeeming the Right to Nominate in our own country, and by having the use of this right shine like a lighthouse before the world, to bring this Age to an end.

Its end can be summed up in nine words:

"The right to nominate belongs to all the people."

Bibliography

Altschuler, Glenn C., and Stuart M. Blumin. *Rude Republic: Americans and Their Politics in the Nineteenth Century.* Princeton, NJ: Princeton University Press, 2000.

Brookhiser, Richard. *Founding Father: Rediscovering George Washington.* New York: Free Press Paperbacks / Simon & Schuster, 1996.

Carson, Clarence B. *A Basic History of the United States.* Vol. 2, *The Beginning of the Republic, 1775–1825.* Wadley, AL: American Textbook Committee, 1984.

Chernow, Ron. *Alexander Hamilton.* New York: The Penguin Press, 2004.

Collier, Christopher, and James Lincoln Collier. *Decision in Philadelphia: The Constitutional Convention of 1787.* New York: Ballantine Books, 1986.

The Constitution of the United States of America.

De Tocqueville, Alexis. *Democracy in America and Two Essays on America.* Translated by Gerald E. Bevan. Notes by Isaac Kramnick. London: Penguin Books, 2003.

Dunn, Susan. *Jefferson's Second Revolution: The Election Crisis of 1800 and the Triumph of Republicanism.* Boston: Houghton Mifflin Company, 2004.

Ellis, Joseph J. *American Creation: Triumphs and Tragedies at the Founding of the Republic.* New York: Alfred A. Knopf, 2007.

———. *American Sphinx: The Character of Thomas Jefferson.* New York: Vintage Books, 1998.

———. *Founding Brothers: The Revolutionary Generation.* New York: Vintage Books, 2002

———. *His Excellency: George Washington.* New York: Alfred A. Knopf, 2004.

Halliday, E. M. *Understanding Thomas Jefferson.* New York: Perennial / HarperCollins Publishers, 2001.

Hamilton, Alexander, James Madison, and John Jay. *The Federalist: The Famous Papers on the Principles of American Government.* Edited by Benjamin F. Wright. New York: Barnes & Noble Books, 2004.

Hutson, James H., ed. *The Founders on Religion: A Book of Quotations.* Princeton, NJ: Princeton University Press, 2005.

Kaminski, John P. *The Founders on the Founders: Word Portraits from the American Revolutionary Era.* Charlottesville: University of Virginia Press, 2008.

Ketcham, Ralph, ed. *The Anti-Federalist Papers and the Constitutional Convention Debates: The Clashes and the Compromises that Gave Birth to Our Form of Government.* New York: New American Library, 1986.

Madison, James. *Notes of Debates in the Federal Convention of 1787 Reported by James Madison.* Introduced by Adrienne Koch. New York: W. W. Norton & Company, 1987.

Mapp, Alf J., Jr. *The Faiths of Our Fathers: What America's Founders Really Believed.* New York: Barnes & Noble, Inc., 2006. First published 2003 by Rowman & Littlefield Publishers, Inc.

McCullough, David. *John Adams*. New York: Touchstone / Simon & Schuster, 2001.

Melton, Buckner F., Jr., ed. *The Quotable Founding Fathers: A Treasury of 2,500 Wise and Witty Quotations from the Men and Women Who Created America*. New York: Fall River Press, 2008.

Morgan, Edmund S. *American Heroes: Profiles of Men and Women Who Shaped Early America*. New York: W. W. Norton & Company, 2009.

———. *The Genuine Article: A Historian Looks at Early America*. New York: W. W. Norton & Company, 2004.

Platt, Suzy, ed. *Respectfully Quoted: A Dictionary of Quotations*. New York: Barnes & Noble Books, 1993.

Waldman, Steven. *Founding Faith: Providence, Politics and the Birth of Religious Freedom in America*. New York: Random House, 2008.

Wills, Garry. *James Madison*. The American Presidents Series. New York: Times Books, 2002.

Wood, Gordon S. *The Creation of the American Republic, 1776–1787*. Chapel Hill: The University of North Carolina Press, 1998. Published for the Omohundro Institute of Early American History and Culture at Williamsburg, Virginia.

Acknowledgements

The author wishes to say: "Although I've criticized certain failures on the part of modern historians, I also must acknowledge that I owe an enormous debt to them for their work. Without them none of us would know the first thing about our country's history, and this book could not have been written. Thank you."

With special thanks to:

Joseph Ellis
Ron Chernow
David McCullough
E.M. Halliday
Steven Waldman
John Kaminski
Edmund Morgan
Richard Brookhiser

Personal Thanks:

To my lovely wife Cynthia for her patience and godliness over many years; to our five children, the best children on earth; to their wives and husbands, equally great; and to our grandchildren. To my wonderful daughter, Amy, whose professionalism contributed so greatly, and to son-in-law Peter, for his early, spot-on review. To many friends, for their support; to Josh Farmer for his brilliant cover design and for his wide knowledge of publishing, who helped greatly to reshape my manuscript.

Thanks to Jake Weidmann for permission to use his amazing artwork, "Eagle and Anchor"; and to my first editor James Jankowiak, who gave not only invaluable correction and advice, but also the encouragement of a friend. Greatest thanks go to our greatest friend and Lord, Jesus Christ.

(continued from back cover)

After his schooling, Mr. Peterson intended to pursue the life of a philosopher, but felt the call to ministry and thus spent several decades serving as a senior pastor, regional overseer, and international teacher. During his years of service and leadership in the church setting, Mr. Peterson's political insight and awe for the republic the Founding Fathers originally designed remained constant, even as his motivation grew to see the fullness of its potential glory and justice benefit the American people.

Thomas and his wife Cynthia make their home in Kansas City near three of their five children, all of whom are involved in their communities, military service, careers, and in the fight against human trafficking, respectively.

Printed in the United States
By Bookmasters